CW00521525

Advance Praise for *Disruptive Strategies*

"*Disruptive Strategies* captures the essence of military campaigns while remaining sensitive to the uniqueness of each and the complex causality of events. The reader will deepen his or her appreciation both for the interactive nature of war and the importance of identifying and exploiting shifts in the character of warfare. This book will help readers mature their own theory of war, gain a deeper appreciation for essential elements of success in war, and, perhaps most important, think clearly about how to deter war by anticipating evolutions in the means by which adversaries may intend to wage it. The editor and contributors are to be congratulated for producing compelling history relevant to contemporary issues of national security."

—H. R. McMaster, author of *Battlegrounds: The Fight to Defend the Free World*

"David Berkey has edited a wonderful study by a number of eminent strategic and military historians on the response by major powers to the threats posed by emergent powers. It represents a nuanced, intelligent discussion of what the past suggests about how American strategists need to think about the rise of the People's Republic of China with its military and economic power."

—Williamson Murray, professor emeritus, Ohio State University, and Marshall Professor, Marine Corps University

"The routine way to describe the contributors to this splendid book would be as 'distinguished scholars,' but each is far more than that: an interesting thinker able to communicate provocative insights with unfashionable clarity. Engaging with topics that range from ancient wars in the Mediterranean through early modern strategic upheaval in northern Europe and on into a projected East Asian future, the authors make history immediate and its lessons sharply relevant. It is rare, nowadays, to encounter a volume so compact yet so rich in thought."

—Ralph Peters, author of *Cain at Gettysburg* and *Lines of Fire*

DISRUPTIVE STRATEGIES

The Hoover Institution gratefully acknowledges the following individuals and foundations for their significant support of the WORKING GROUP ON THE ROLE OF MILITARY HISTORY IN CONTEMPORARY CONFLICT:

Martin Anderson

The Lynde & Harry Bradley Foundation

Pilar and Lew Davies

William L. Edwards and Marienne Emblad

The Bertha and John Garabedian
    Charitable Foundation

James and Daphne Jameson

Jennifer L. "Jenji" Mercer

Rebekah Mercer

Roger and Martha Mertz

Jeremiah Milbank III

Victor S. Trione

DISRUPTIVE STRATEGIES

The Military Campaigns
of Ascendant Powers
and Their Rivals

Edited by David L. Berkey

HOOVER INSTITUTION PRESS

STANFORD UNIVERSITY   STANFORD, CALIFORNIA

With its eminent scholars and world-renowned library and archives, the Hoover Institution seeks to improve the human condition by advancing ideas that promote economic opportunity and prosperity, while securing and safeguarding peace for America and all mankind. The views expressed in its publications are entirely those of the authors and do not necessarily reflect the views of the staff, officers, or Board of Overseers of the Hoover Institution.

hoover.org

Hoover Institution Press Publication No. 712

Hoover Institution at Leland Stanford Junior University,
Stanford, California 94305-6003

Copyright © 2021 by the Board of Trustees of the
Leland Stanford Junior University
All rights reserved. No part of this publication may be reproduced, stored in a retrieval system, or transmitted in any form or by any means, electronic, mechanical, photocopying, recording, or otherwise, without written permission of the publisher and copyright holders.

For permission to reuse material from *Disruptive Strategies: The Military Campaigns of Ascendant Powers and Their Rivals*, ISBN 978-0-8179-2384-6, please access copyright.com or contact the Copyright Clearance Center, Inc. (CCC), 222 Rosewood Drive, Danvers, MA 01923, 978-750-8400. CCC is a not-for-profit organization that provides licenses and registration for a variety of uses.

First printing 2021
27 26 25 24 23 22 21   7 6 5 4 3 2 1

Manufactured in the United States of America
Printed on acid-free, archival-quality paper

Library of Congress Cataloging-in-Publication Data

Names: Berkey, David L. (David Langford), editor.
Title: Disruptive strategies : the military campaigns of ascendant powers and their rivals / edited by David L. Berkey.
Description: Stanford, California : Hoover Institution Press, Stanford University, 2021. | Includes bibliographical references and index. | Summary: "Historians analyze military campaigns between dominant states and the rising powers who challenge them, from the ancient era to a hypothetical future"—Provided by publisher.
Identifiers: LCCN 2020039359 (print) | LCCN 2020039360 (ebook) | ISBN 9780817923846 (cloth) | ISBN 9780817923860 (epub) | ISBN 9780817923877 (mobi) | ISBN 9780817923884 (pdf)
Subjects: LCSH: Military history. | Strategy—History. | Military policy—History.
Classification: LCC D25.5 .D57 2021 (print) | LCC D25.5 (ebook) | DDC 355.4/8—dc23
LC record available at https://lccn.loc.gov/2020039359
LC ebook record available at https://lccn.loc.gov/2020039360

CONTENTS

FOREWORD

*Working Group on the Role of
Military History in Contemporary Conflict
at the Hoover Institution, Stanford University*

In 2012 the former director of the Hoover Institution, Dr. John Raisian, asked me to establish a working group of American and international military historians and analysts to study contemporary strategic dilemmas and military crises in the context of military history. At the time, the recent wars in Afghanistan, Iraq, Libya, and Syria; the collapsing reset relations with Russia; radical Islamist terrorist attacks within the United States; tensions with China over the militarization of the Spratly Islands; ongoing unrest in the Middle East; worries over the nuclear ambitions of Iran; and the dangerous reality of North Korea as a nuclear power all called for reasoned analysis. But they also called for scrutiny guided by the perspective and wisdom of the past, given that all those areas have had long experiences with war, often over the same political and religious fault lines as in the present age.

We were tasked with assembling a diverse group of historians, scholars, popular commentators, and former military and political officials. What followed was the creation of the Working Group on the Role of Military History in Contemporary Conflict, whose official mission statement was to examine how knowledge of past military operations can influence contemporary public-policy decisions concerning current conflicts. The purpose then was to offer guidance to policy makers and the public, not just to engage in historical debate—as needed as that is for the advance of a critical scholarly discipline.

The Military History Working Group (MHWG), as it is informally called, has published sixty-five consecutive issues of its online journal *Strategika*, which focuses on topics of current history (e.g., an ascendant China, the waning presence of the United States in the Middle East, nationalism versus globalism) but, again, analyzed in the context of the past. One of the group's working assumptions is that human nature does not change much across time and place. With proper allowances for radical industrial and technological transformations of the modern world, looking back at the Peloponnesian War, the Crusades, or World War I can reassure the public that we are not alone and that prior generations endured the same sorts of war, plague, and terrorism that we suffer in the twenty-first century.

Many of the discussions during the group's biannual meetings have provided the topics and narratives of *Strategika*. Every month, the journal explores a contemporary military or strategic challenge in the news through two short contrasting essays and a longer historical background that draws on past events to elucidate the topic in a wider framework. The issue also includes several short opinion pieces from group members, a poll of readers about possible solutions to these challenges, and topics for further study.

In addition to the MHWG's meetings and the publication of *Strategika*, we publish "Military History in the News" on the Hoover Institution's website (https://www.hoover.org/publications/military-history-news). These are short editorials, published four times every month—more than two hundred to date—connecting ongoing crises (e.g., the COVID-19 outbreak and Chinese culpability, dissension in NATO, or the strategic agendas of Russia) with similar episodes in history.

In addition, "Classics of Military History" (https://www.hoover.org/publications/classics-military-history) offers an ongoing online catalogue of short book reviews by group members who briefly analyze the contemporary value and influence of some of the great military histories and analyses of the past (e.g., Thucydides, *Peloponnesian War*; Niccolò Machiavelli, *The Art of War*; and Henry Kissinger, *Nuclear Weapons and Foreign Policy*). We now have assembled more than sixty titles that are posted for readers to consult.

As part of these various projects to bring military history out of the shadows for students, scholars, the general public, and public officials and politicians, we now are inaugurating a new book series, drawing on contributions from MHWG scholars and edited by *Strategika* managing editor and group member Dr. David L. Berkey.

This inaugural volume, *Disruptive Strategies: The Military Campaigns of Ascendant Powers and Their Rivals*, reviews rivalries from the classical world to the twenty-first century. One focus of the authors is the current rise of the People's Republic of China, which not only has been candid about proclaiming that it will shortly become the world's new hegemon but also reminds its rivals that the existing family of nations—especially the United States, Europe, and the Westernized states of the so-called free world—should accept this inevitable reality and thus make the necessary concessions and adjustments to a changing global order.

The rise of Chinese power and influence is especially germane as I write in May 2020. The COVID-19 viral epidemic, which appeared in early 2020, has led to hundreds of thousands of deaths worldwide as well as a veritable global shutdown and ensuing severe world recession. The virus originated in Wuhan, China. It likely could have been contained in initial local manifestations had not the Chinese government—apparently worried over possible economic losses and forfeit of global prestige—hidden the virus's origins, its rates of infectiousness, and the real dangers of the disease's spreading to the world community.

As a result, China was widely blamed for the disaster by nations reeling from the human, medical, and economic costs of the epidemic. Beijing's once supposed foreordained ascendance was put in doubt, given the determination of countries to readjust radically their commercial and trade relations with China, and, although belatedly, to seek deterrence against its pre-virus military buildup.

The contributors to this volume, whose essays were presented for publication in advance of the epidemic, remind us that none of the current global players, both ascending and waning powers, are engaged in a novel contest. They compete in an ancient pattern of rivalry in which nations do not necessarily become world powers by some predetermined trajectory but do so rather by a series of often unforeseen human and natural events, by poor or inspired leadership, or through critical prior economic and military choices often not appreciated as pivotal at the time they were made.

The rises and falls of powers are not inevitable occurrences. Nor must big-power rivalries lead to war. Instead events occur from decisions that peoples and their government make, whether they are aware of the real consequences or not. In sum, the current volume helps to remind us of the role of free will—and that none of us are the captives to fixed forces beyond our comprehension and our power to alter.

VICTOR DAVIS HANSON
Martin and Illie Anderson Senior Fellow, Classics and
    Military History
Hoover Institution, Stanford University
Chair, Working Group on the Role of Military History
    in Contemporary Conflict

ACKNOWLEDGMENTS

This volume of essays had its genesis during a conversation with Ralph Peters at one of the biannual meetings of the Hoover Working Group on the Role of Military History in Contemporary Conflict. He drew my attention to the usual focus of numerous studies of famous battles on tactics and operations, but at the expense of strategic analyses—the primary concern of our working group of military historians and national security analysts at the Hoover Institution. With the support of Victor Davis Hanson, without whom none of our work would be possible, the project then received the enthusiastic encouragement of Denise Elson, Hoover's associate director of research operations, and Christopher S. Dauer, Hoover's associate director of marketing and strategic communications. I am also extremely grateful to Hoover's director, Thomas Gilligan, for allowing us the ability to pursue Hoover themes that, in the words of our Institution's founder Herbert Hoover, "recall the voice of experience against the making of war, and by the study of these records and their publication, to recall man's endeavors to make and preserve peace, and to sustain for America the safeguards of the American way of life." In addition, my friend and colleague Bruce S. Thornton provided valuable advice at the outset of this project. At the Hoover Press, I would like to thank the outstanding team of Barbara Arellano, Marshall Blanchard, Danica Michels Hodge, Mike Iveson, Rebecca Logan, Victoria Taylor and her team at International Mapping Associates for the production of the maps in this book, and Howie Severson for the cover design. They were a pleasure to work with throughout the entire process of taking a rough manuscript to a finished publication.

As a private organization, the Hoover Institution relies upon the generosity of its donors to foster the work of its scholars and the dissemination of their scholarship. I would like to thank those specific individuals and organizations who have helped to fund our work, in particular Martin Anderson, Pilar and Lew Davies, William L. Edwards and Marienne Emblad, James and Daphne Jameson, Jennifer L. "Jenji" Mercer, Rebekah Mercer, Roger and Martha Mertz, Jeremiah Milbank III, Victor S. Trione, the Bertha and John Garabedian Charitable Foundation, and the Lynde & Harry Bradley Foundation.

Last, I would like express my personal gratitude for the decades of support that I have received from my mentors, Donald Kagan, who was my graduate adviser at Yale University, and Victor Davis Hanson, for whom I have the greatest admiration for his work as a scholar and his guidance as a friend. It has been my privilege to learn from both of them.

INTRODUCTION

David L. Berkey

After the United States spent nearly two decades focusing on non-state terrorist actors, the publication of the National Security Strategy in December 2017 signaled a recalibration of American foreign and military policy to confront the growing threats of former Cold War foes: "A belief emerged, among many, that American power would be unchallenged and self-sustaining. The United States began to drift. We experienced a crisis of confidence and surrendered our advantages in key areas. As we took our political, economic, and military advantages for granted, other actors steadily implemented their long-term plans to challenge America and to advance agendas opposed to the United States, our allies, and our partners. . . . China and Russia challenge American power, influence, and interests, attempting to erode American security and prosperity."[1]

Today, the competition between the United States and China is far more than a race to amass the greatest arsenal of military assets—a competition in which the United States continues to maintain its lead against all foes in both quantitative and qualitative terms. The rivalry also encompasses global trade and economic influence, the role of epidemic outbreaks, artificial intelligence, space, cyberspace, and fintech (financial technology). At its core is a struggle between nations with competing ideologies, antithetical systems of government, and irreconcilable visions of global governance.

The present volume is a product of the Hoover Institution's Working Group on the Role of Military History in Contemporary

Conflict at Stanford University. Formed by Victor Davis Hanson in 2012, the group set out to examine how knowledge of past military operations can influence contemporary public-policy decisions concerning current conflicts. To address this mission, and specifically in light of the challenge that China poses to American interests, I assembled the present group of distinguished scholars to identify and discuss military campaigns from two different angles: one, in which hegemonic states confronted rising powers seeking to topple them, or two, conversely, in which rising powers contested the leadership of a dominant state.

Five of the six chapters in this volume analyze military campaigns from classical antiquity to the Napoleonic era, with the last an imagined scenario of a hypothetical conflict between the United States and China fought in the East and South China Seas. All of the past campaigns described were fought in the western hemisphere. What emerges is a wide array of viewpoints concerning the importance of military strategy, the structure of power in the interstate arena, the relative strengths of competing states, and the influence of leadership. Within general parameters, the authors were given the freedom to approach the topic of rising power competition as they wished, and their contributions demonstrate a variety of creative approaches.

The locus classicus for the study of rising powers and their rivals is the conflict between Athens and Sparta in the fifth century BCE (431–404/3), known as the Peloponnesian War, which the historian Thucydides recounted "to be a possession for all time and not just a performance-piece for the moment."[2] He believed that it was "the greatest ever upheaval among the Greeks, and one which affected a good part of the barbarian world too—even, you could say, most of mankind" and that "earlier events were not on the same scale, either as regards their wars or in other respects."[3] Thucydides was not content merely to narrate the events of this war; he also wanted to reflect upon the causes that had brought it to pass. Distinguishing between the immediate and the real or "truest" cause of the war, he wrote: "I consider the truest cause, though the one least openly stated, to be this: the Athenians were becoming powerful and inspired fear in the Spartans and so forced them into war."[4] Debate arises whether Thucydides's famous assessment belies his own contrary evidence of innate and irreconcilable differences (democracy/oligarchy, Ionian/Dorian, sea power/land power, cosmopolitanism/parochialism, chattel slavery/helotage) between Athens and Sparta that had already prompted a long and earlier war (460–445 BCE).

Given Thucydides's view of unchanging human nature and the current assessment of today's threat environment, it is alarming to think that war between the United States and China might be inevitable. Graham Allison explored this determinist proposition in *Destined for War: Can America and China Escape Thucydides's Trap?* (New York: Houghton Mifflin Harcourt, 2017), in which he undertakes an empirical study involving sixteen historical examples of rising powers attempting to displace ruling ones, concluding that twelve ended in violence. In the other four instances where war was avoided, imaginative statecraft was the solution.

The current essays, of course, all illustrate examples where states have elected to go to war. In this respect, the present volume seeks to examine both the military responses of hegemons to threats to their predominant status, as well as those of rising powers seeking to challenge the established order. For this reason, the word *ascendant* as employed in the title of this collection of historical studies refers to states that have recently achieved perceived dominance as well as those growing in strength and influence in an agenda to achieve superiority. The use of the term *campaign*—defined in the *Oxford English Dictionary* as "the continuance and operations of an army 'in the field' for a season or other definite portion of time, or while engaged in one continuous series of military operations constituting the whole, or a distinct part, of a war"[5]—also needs clarification. The reference is broad in the temporal sense, extending from a single year, as in the case of Napoleon's Italian campaign of 1796, all the way to the struggle between Rome and Carthage, which lasted over a century from 264 to 146 BCE. Unlike studies of particular battles that emphasize operational tactics, the examples all elucidate states' calculus in combining resources and the force necessary to attain their strategic goals.

The successes of many of the campaigns described in this book were short-lived, and the powers that achieved them were often unable to consolidate their gains. This was certainly the case with the Greek city-states of the fifth century BCE. The same could also be said of the efforts of Gustavus Adolphus and Napoleon. In contrast, Rome's victories over Carthage in the Punic Wars as well as those of the Byzantine Empire against the Sasanids illustrate the long-lasting effects of successfully executed military campaigns. Such diversity of these past conflicts emphasizes the challenges that ascendant powers faced in their risky quest for hegemony and the conditions required to maintain it.

In considering the outbreak of war between the Greek world's two most powerful poleis of the fifth century BCE, ascendant Sparta and rising Athens, Paul A. Rahe begins his analysis with the Greco-Persian Wars (490–479 BCE), the period during and immediately after which Athens constructed both its fleet and municipal fortifications, and thereby embraced an agenda of imperial power. Ambitious leadership within two such antithetical states either to hold or become the hegemonic power in Greece led to a bitter rivalry that lasted decades and culminated with the outbreak of full-scale war from 431 to 404 BCE, the Peloponnesian War—and eventually the defeat of Athens and the dissolution of its empire.

Rahe demonstrates how the differing advantages of Athens and Sparta—the former with a dominant navy and the latter with unsurpassed infantry—created opportunities at times for each to exploit the weaknesses of its adversary. Unforeseen circumstances throughout the fifth century (e.g., the devastating Laconian earthquake of 464 BCE and the Athenian plague of 430 BCE), overextension (e.g., the Athenians' expeditions to Egypt in 459–454 BCE and Sicily in 415–413 BCE), and the Spartans' ambivalence about decisively subjugating the Athenians during the interval between the Greco-Persian and Peloponnesian Wars contributed to an impasse and uneasy balance of power that would only eventually swing in favor of Sparta with Persia's support. Rahe challenges the traditional view of the bipolar structure of the state system consisting of Athens and its allies on the one hand and Sparta and its allies on the other, seeing it instead as tripolar with the inclusion of the much larger and wealthier Persian Empire situated on the periphery of the Greek world and capable of opportunistically using its vast powers to influence affairs in Greece in its own perceived self-interest. In summation, an eventual Spartan commitment to force decisive action and a willingness to draw upon the considerable resources of a former foreign rival brought about the defeat of Athens—but not until the two major combatants exhausted their populations after nearly three decades of war.

Barry Strauss examines another classical conflict in focusing on the three wars fought between Carthage and Rome in the third and second centuries BCE, known collectively as the Punic Wars (264–146). This long period of intermittent and intercontinental armed rivalry began as a Roman effort in Sicily to stem the potential threat that Carthage might pose to the security of the entire Italian peninsula. Then, in a second and later phase, the war shifted to Carthage's efforts in southern Spain to aggregate enough power to invade Roman Italy itself. The two sides enlisted a variety of their allies, in an eventual existential struggle between the two great powers of the western Mediterranean that ended in a third and final interval with the annihilation of Carthage itself. As Strauss explains, both Rome and Carthage were ambitious military rivals that ostensibly had much in common as agrarian, oligarchic states. Yet there were significant differences as well that ultimately would prove decisive. For example, Carthage employed mercenaries, and was less effective in its management of allies than was Rome. While Carthage initially had an advantage in the experience and skill of its generals, Rome proved adept in marshaling superior manpower, and eventually found commanders such as Metellus, Fabius, and Scipio comparable or superior to their Carthaginian counterparts.

Strauss reaches several important conclusions that are relevant to the current rivalry between the United States and China. Rome and Carthage, for example, were both rising powers that sought to expand their spheres of regional influence that made conflict likely when Carthage's expansion threatened Roman territorial interests. The Romans were ultimately victorious in part due to their diplomatic skills and abilities both in negotiating and preserving alliances and in fielding armies of free citizens that had a stake in republican government. More generally, Strauss demonstrates how it is vital to appreciate the undeniable strengths of the enemy while searching out its weaknesses—and to then be prepared to exploit those vulnerabilities. He also argues it is critical to anticipate and counter with superior skill and resources the enemy's preferred manner of combat, and in times of crisis to maintain cohesiveness in governance and close coordination between political and military leadership.

In the following chapter, Edward N. Luttwak also focuses on two great imperial powers, the Byzantine Empire and its nemesis the Sasanian Empire, the successor to the Parthian Empire and the last great Iranian kingdom before the conquests of Islamic armies of the mid-seventh century CE. In contrast to Strauss's investigation of the entirety of the more-than-a-century-long duration of the three Punic Wars, Luttwak confines his study of the protracted rivalry between the two empires to the single military campaign launched by the Byzantine emperor Herakleios in 627, a dramatic victory that resulted in the death of the ruling Sasanian monarch, Khosrow II, in 628 and paved the way for the subsequent downfall of the Sasanian Empire itself shortly thereafter.

While the Roman and successive Byzantine Empires had fought the Sasanians for centuries, a balance of power had emerged and the combatants had more or less refrained from attempts to annihilate each other. That uneasy arrangement changed in 603 when Khosrow II began a war to topple the reigning Byzantine emperor, Phokas (r. 602–610), and to absorb his weakened empire. After years of continued military successes, the Sasanians had conquered the Byzantine Empire's valuable holdings in Egypt and pushed them all the way back to the walls of Constantinople.

Under these dire circumstances, Phokas's successor, Herakleios, led a counteroffensive against the Sasanians to save and later to expand his empire. Leaving Constantinople behind, Herakleios set off into the heart of the Sasanian Empire in what Luttwak describes as "a high-risk, relational maneuver on a theater-wide scale—an historical rarity in military history, with no comparable precedents or subsequent examples." Luttwak draws our attention again to the importance of alliances, this time a long-dormant partnership with a Turkic steppe power that supplied Herakleios with forty thousand soldiers. Khosrow—overextended with his forces deployed as far away as Egypt and the gates of Constantinople—miscalculated both the threat that Herakleios posed to the Sasanian heartland and the Byzantines' bold resolve to attack his palatial complexes at Nineveh, Dastagird, and Ctesiphon. Those miscalculations proved to be fatal.

Herakleios provides us with an example of the importance of taking calculated risks, even when conventional wisdom suggests that a beleaguered power should not return to the offensive. As Luttwak makes clear, Herakleios's genius and daring in discovering the weaknesses within Sasanian offensive operations were instrumental in saving the Byzantine Empire from ruin. In a similar fashion, the next two chapters—likewise highlighting individual genius in the careers of both Gustavus Adolphus and Napoleon—also draw our attention to the critical role of a single military leader, whose skills at times can surpass even considerations of geography, manpower, resources, and technology.

In the fourth chapter, Peter R. Mansoor describes the abrupt rise of Sweden in the early seventeenth century, a local power that previously had played a limited role in regional politics. The emergence of the warrior king Gustavus Adolphus—educated, energetic, and respected by his people—ushered in a new era of greater Swedish influence in Europe for the impoverished nation. In addition to economic, financial, industrial, and personnel reforms, Gustavus brought about a revolution in military affairs with the creation of linear formations along with combined-arms warfare, making the Swedish military one of Europe's most lethal when it entered the Thirty Years' War in 1630. Bolstered with money from an opportunistic alliance with France spearheaded by Cardinal Richelieu, Gustavus invaded northern Germany to reduce perceived threats posed by the Holy Roman Empire's domination of the Baltic.

With each victory on the continent (e.g., Werben, Breitenfeld), Sweden acquired the added funds to extend further its campaign. Without continued victories and the accompanying profits, the survival of the campaign was impossible. In 1632, at the Battle of Lützen, Swedish forces won a narrow victory but suffered the loss of Gustavus. The death of their leader, combined with the emulation of Sweden's tactics by opposing Holy Roman imperial forces, now reversed the Swedes' fortune. The new commander, Chancellor Oxenstierna, was eventually able to extricate Sweden from the conflict (Treaty of Prague, 1635)—only to return to the continent shortly again with French assistance, and win pivotal battles. As a result, by 1645, Sweden was a true regional power and remained so until the end of the century. Mansoor concludes with the reminder that "inspired leadership is not a substitute for an effective national security apparatus for crafting sound policy and strategy and applying the full range of state power to achieve desired goals." Gustavus Adolphus won prominence for Sweden, but his successors failed to maintain it, largely because his strategic insight and tactical brilliance were not institutionalized but rested only with the career of a singular leader.

Andrew Roberts focuses on the expansion of French power during Napoleon's campaign against Austrian forces in Italy, especially in the single year from March 1796 to March 1797. Napoleon's multifarious objectives in the Italian campaign were to increase security along France's southern border, to plunder northern Italy and restore the depleted French treasury, to punish his archenemy Austria, and to spread revolutionary ardor to areas outside of France in hopes of undermining the monarchies of his many enemies. Napoleon, of course, also sought victory for his own material aggrandizement and, psychologically, to establish his military reputation as an invincible and popular catalyst of radical change. After his arrival to command the expedition and his careful attention to his own soldiers' morale, provisions, and equipment, Napoleon relied on his customary speed and deception to defeat his enemy's numerically superior forces. Roberts argues that Napoleon's military success in Italy was due to his employment of a wide array of inspired tactics that kept his opponents confused and at a constant operational disadvantage. In the Italian campaign, we have a clear example of the benefits conferred by Napoleonic generalship, itself the result of focused education, endless training, and innate intelligence.

The final chapter offers a thought experiment of a putative military campaign that has not, and one hopes will not, occur. Michael R. Auslin explores a hypothetical conflict, which he calls the "Sino-American Littoral War," fought between the People's Republic of China and the United States and its allies in the year 2025 over contested areas of the East and South China Seas. Auslin constructs a likely worsening political scenario predicated on deteriorating contemporary US-China relations. He inventories the two nations' respective military assets, and then imagines the war's outbreak after a series of accidental preliminary encounters, initially an aerial collision resulting in the loss of both an American EP-3 reconnaissance plane and a Chinese J-20 fighter, as well as a naval collision that damages a US Coast Guard cutter. With tensions rising and diplomacy failing, China then begins to escalate from resolvable skirmishes to a regional war, but in ways still designed to limit the scope of the fighting by ensuring a favorable outcome before the inevitable arrival of superior US naval reinforcements.

In our context of analyzing ascendant powers and their wary adversaries, China seeks to fragment the Western alliance in the Pacific by creating tensions among Japan, South Korea, Taiwan, the Philippines, and Australia, as one way of neutralizing the otherwise overwhelmingly superior military forces at the disposal of the United States. The idea of a mutually limited confrontation between the United States and China is emphasized by recognition that both nuclear powers rightly fear the trajectory of escalating conflict. Nonetheless, given these parameters, China still seeks to control to its advantage commercial navigation in the East and South China Seas, to reunite Taiwan to mainland China, and to undermine the influence of the United States in the region, as a precursor to displacing America entirely from Asia. In Auslin's scenario, in order to resolve what seems initially as a manageable and limited conflict, the president of the United States understandably has made various concessions to Chinese leadership that wrongly have given the impression that China won a war with an established and superior rival power far more fearful than Beijing of igniting an all-out war. Auslin, nonetheless, suggests that even an ascendant China's relations with nations in the region will be intrinsically limited by stark ideological differences that make sustained and symmetrical economic and political cooperation almost impossible with them. Meanwhile, in Auslin's scenario, the United States will rebound to expand and enhance both its national defense capabilities vis-à-vis China and its own outreach to natural allies in the region. Without the possibility of any clear-cut winner, such regional confrontations simply reflect what will likely become a continued Cold War, with neither side seeing the benefits of absolute victory at the high cost of war between two large, rich, technologically sophisticated, and nuclear rivals.

From these six examples—five historical and one hypothetical—we are left with a number of warnings and lessons about the dangers of ascendant powers and the responses they incur from their intended targets. For a rising challenger, such as the Athenians and the Sasanians, ambitious expansion can become counterproductive, at least if newly ambitious agendas exceed a state's existing capabilities and the ascendant power ignores the role of third parties that so often coalesce against a recognized aggressor. This is especially true for a state that is relatively unproven and unacquainted with the responsibilities of regional or continental hegemony.

Sparta's alliance with the Persians and the Byzantine Empire's outreach to Turkic steppe peoples were as unexpected as they were successful in arresting the rise of Athens and the Sasanian Empire, respectively. In the cases of Gustavus Adolphus and Napoleon, spectacular success hinged on superior high command and innovative tactics that were unfortunately not always characteristic of either the Swedish or French military. Eventually, limitations in the human and financial resources of both Sweden and France, along with their enemies' emulative adoption of newly developed tactics, restored a balance of power.

In both the cases of Carthage and a rising China, the provocative measures necessary to extend their ambitions into previously contested buffer zones demanded responses from Rome and the United States. And both Rome and the United States were far more adept at nurturing alliances than were their adversaries. They enjoyed far more extensive resources, and felt that their national security interests in the disputed areas were existential and tied to their own safety and survival. Ultimately, Rome triumphed, and the long-term outcome of the hypothetical war between China and the United States was uncertain. We are left to contemplate the many dimensions in which the United States must continue to outpace our adversaries to deter the efforts of a rising state to supplant our global leadership.

NOTES

1. White House, National Security Strategy of the United States of America (December 2017), 2. https://www.whitehouse.gov/wp-content/uploads/2017/12/NSS-Final-12-18-2017-0905.pdf.
2. Thucydides 1.22.4. This and the following translations of Thucydides are from Jeremy Mynott, ed. and trans., *Thucydides: The War of the Peloponnesians and the Athenians* (Cambridge: Cambridge University Press, 2013).
3. Thucydides 1.1.2 and 1.1.3, respectively.
4. Thucydides 1.23.6.
5. "Campaign, n. 3. Military." OED Online. Oxford University Press.

1

SPARTA ASCENDANT, ATHENS RISING: ALLIANCE, AMBIVALENCE, RIVALRY, AND WAR IN A TRIPOLAR WORLD

Paul A. Rahe

Great quarrels, it has been said, often arise from small occasions but never from small causes.
—Winston S. Churchill[1]

When an invasion, constituting an existential threat, is turned back, the victors celebrate, as they have every right to do. Then, however, when the euphoria wears off, they begin to rethink their situation and to reconsider their options—as also do those who lost and those who kept their distance from the fray. Moreover, when the victorious party is made up of a coalition of more or less equal partners, the coalition itself soon comes into question—especially when the threat posed by the defeated party has vanished or receded. Only rarely do coalitions of this sort long outlast the danger that inspired their formation and provided the adhesive holding them together.

The Hellenic League is a case in point. It was formed against Persia in or shortly before 481 BCE by Sparta, Athens, and various lesser powers already to one degree or another within the orbit of the two dominant partners. In 480, thanks in large part to the canniness of Themistocles and the size of the Athenian fleet, this coalition achieved a decisive naval victory at Salamis over Xerxes,

the Achaemenid monarch of Persia's vast empire. Then, in 479, thanks in large part to the cunning and courage of the Spartans, it annihilated that Great King's army at Plataea. The victory that this alliance won on that same day at Mycale, opposite Samos on the western coast of Anatolia, served to confirm the results secured at Salamis and Plataea and guaranteed that the ruler whom the Greeks sometimes called "the Mede" would not in the immediate future return.[2]

Initially, as one would expect, there was a burst of camaraderie. But it did not take long for the two main powers in the league to begin eyeing one another warily. The size of the fleet that Athens had managed to deploy and the skill displayed at Salamis by the crews who manned its triremes had in 480 been a consolation to its Aeginetan and Corinthian neighbors and allies. But after Plataea and Mycale, when Persia ceased to be an immediate threat, this force came to be seen as a source of concern. In consequence, emissaries from Aegina and almost certainly Corinth as well were dispatched to the Spartans at Lacedaemon in the late summer or fall of 479 to urge that it step in to prevent their Athenian allies from rebuilding the city walls that the Achaemenid king's Persians had torn down. It was, they thought, essential that, if Athens was to be supreme at sea, it remain vulnerable on land.[3]

The Lacedaemonians, who were landlubbers, may well have been less sensitive to the threat posed by Athens's maritime supremacy than were the Aeginetans and Corinthians. But they saw the point, and they were quite responsive to the concerns of their allies within and close by the Peloponnese. They had need of these communities, and this was not apt to change. The little empire that they governed in the southern two-fifths of that great peninsula was fragile. The Spartans, who formed this empire's ruling order, were greatly outnumbered by the servile class of Helots who farmed the allotments from which they drew their sustenance; and a great mountain range divided the Eurotas River valley in Laconia to the east, where this master class resided, from the Pamisos River valley in Messenia to the west, where the land was more fertile and the Helots far more numerous. To sustain control they needed support not only from the perioeci—the free but politically subordinate population that resided in villages on the margins of their territory within these two river valleys—but also from their allies further afield. Otherwise, should there be a Helot revolt (as there had been on more than one occasion in the past), the Argives, their ancestral foe within the Peloponnese, might well seize upon the occasion as an opportunity to reassert within that peninsula the hegemony that the Lacedaemonians had wrested from them in the not-too-distant past.[4]

In consequence, upon learning that the Athenians were assiduously rebuilding their walls, the Spartans sent an embassy to Athens to suggest that, to prevent the Persians from returning and using as a base the fortifications of a Greek city, no *pólis* outside the Peloponnese should be walled. Needless to say, this request caused consternation in Athens. As everyone understood at the time, the rationale presented by the Spartan ambassadors made no strategic sense. There were insuperable logistical obstacles to the Persians' return solely by land. To invade Hellas a second time they would have to be able once again to deploy a merchant fleet sufficient to convey the foodstuffs required by a great army on the march—and this they could not effectively do until and unless they had recovered by military means the supremacy at sea that they had enjoyed at the time of the abortive invasion mounted by Xerxes.[5]

In response, then, to the Spartan recommendation, the Athenians resorted to subterfuge, sending Themistocles to Lacedaemon to obfuscate and delay all proceedings while they worked day and night to raise their walls to a level enabling them to defend the town. Although this bit of diplomatic legerdemain succeeded, the Spartans could still have rallied the forces of the alliance that modern scholars call the Peloponnesian League, and then they could have conducted an unstoppable invasion. Moreover, at the time, Athens was not in a condition to outlast a siege. But the Lacedaemonians did not on this occasion have the heart to stage such an assault. They had only recently fought the Mede alongside the Athenians. Panhellenic sentiment was at a high, and the Spartans were a hesitant lot prone to caution. They could not turn on a dime. In any case, they needed Athens's triremes. In their absence, should Xerxes build a new fleet and attempt a comeback, the Hellenes would not be able to fend off the Mede.[6]

In the aftermath, at Themistocles's instigation, the Athenians fortified the Piraeus peninsula and turned its three harbors into a commercial emporium and a naval base, and they initiated an ongoing trireme-building program designed to guarantee that they would have twenty new galleys available every year. The Lacedaemonians were told that these initiatives were aimed at fending off the Mede, which was no doubt true enough. But Themistocles also had another danger in mind, and he pointedly suggested to his compatriots that, if they were ever attacked by land, they could retreat to the Piraeus and defy all comers with their fleet. Although he did not specify which potential antagonists he had in mind, everyone understood the eventuality that he feared. A quarter of a century prior to the battle of Salamis, the Spartans had on four distinct occasions staged invasions of Attica—aimed at turning Athens into a Lacedaemonian satellite.[7]

THE DELIAN LEAGUE

Lacedaemon had for some decades been the leading power in Greece, and its appointees commanded the forces of the Hellenic League not only on land but also at sea. The latter arrangement, however, soon ceased to be the case. Hereby hangs a tale.

In ordinary circumstances, the Spartans looked for military leadership to their dual monarchy. In keeping with this practice, Leotychidas, the king supplied by the Eurypontid branch of the city's Heraclid royal family, had commanded the coalition navy at Mycale. After the battle, however, he had displayed a decided reluctance to commit the alliance to the defense of the inland communities situated near the Anatolian coast that had responded to the arrival of his fleet by casting off the Persian yoke and petitioning for acceptance into the Hellenic League. Instead, he had

suggested that their populations be moved to the Greek mainland
where they could be resettled in the Argolid, in Boeotia, and in
Thessaly—where cities had ostentatiously flirted with or openly
backed the Mede.

Leotychidas's proposal was folly, suggesting strategic idi-
ocy on his part. The defeat inflicted on Xerxes's forces was for
the Persians only a setback. It did not seriously weaken the Achaemenid realm. The Great King controlled three of the world's
four great river valley civilizations. His kingdom's resources—its
manpower and wealth—beggared the imagination. It would not
be hard for Xerxes to mount another invasion. To cede Ionia to
the Mede would be to accord the Hellenes' greatest antagonist a
staging ground within the Aegean from which to make another
attempt to conquer Greece. Xerxes could only be kept at bay if the
Hellenes retained firm control of this corner of the Mediterranean.
It is this fact that explains why Leotychidas was forced to give
way when the Athenians came to the defense of the interests of
their Ionian kinsmen.[8]

The following year, the Spartans dispatched Pausanias to lead
the Hellenic forces at sea. This man—who was the regent for Leotychidas's Agiad counterpart, the deceased Leonidas's young son
Pleistarchus—had distinguished himself for intelligence, vigor,
and courage when he had led the Hellenic forces on land at Plataea, and he was no less resolute and effective as a blue-water
commander. In the south, he wrested control of Cyprus from the
Persians. In the north, he seized Byzantium. But although his
vigorous prosecution of the ongoing war against the Mede must
have been a welcome contrast to the lack of enterprise and the
deep-seated reluctance displayed by Leotychidas, Pausanias also
evidenced an arrogance and an insolence in his dealings with the
Greeks of the east and Sparta's other allies that gave rise both to
complaints registered with the authorities at Lacedaemon and to
fury in the fleet. The commanders sent out by Lacedaemon were
either behindhand and very nearly useless or so offensive that
they were deemed intolerable.[9]

Lacedaemon's defects proved to be Athens's opportunity. When the islanders turned to the chief Athenian commander Aristides, asking that his compatriots take over the leadership of the Hellenic forces at sea, the old fox indicated Athens's willingness to do so. But, at the same time, he insisted that the islanders first demonstrate to the Spartans that they were no longer willing to serve under Sparta's nominees.

This they did; and, in 477, the islanders and the Athenians formed a new alliance under Athens's leadership, which was slated to function as a substitute for the naval force hitherto fielded by the Hellenic League.[10] About this development, the Spartans were ambivalent. Many regarded it as an affront, and some of these advocated launching a war against Athens. Others regarded the founding of what modern scholars call the Delian League as a great relief.

The Lacedaemonians were for the most part homebodies— wary of wandering far from their fastness in the southern Peloponnese. They were not numerous. At this time, the adult males numbered something like eight thousand. The Helot threat was a constant worry, forcing them to do everything within their ability to conserve manpower and to concentrate it at home, where it was most apt to be needed. They also worried that the extreme discipline and public-spiritedness for which they were famous was a hothouse flower that would wither if they were dispersed abroad, and they knew that without these qualities they could neither sustain their way of life nor maintain their dominion over the Helots.

Pausanias's misconduct was as much a matter of concern at Lacedaemon as it was an offense abroad, and there was reason to suspect that, while at Byzantium, he had begun an intrigue with the Mede. Spartan nervousness in this regard was further heightened a year or two thereafter when Leotychidas was caught taking a bribe while commanding an army sent to Thessaly against Persia's local collaborators, the "Medizers" of that fertile, well-watered region. The war at sea needed prosecution. This the Spartans understood. It and only it stood in the way of a Persian resurgence. But it was, many a Lacedaemonian concluded, best left to the Athenians—who were better situated and more than eager to take it on.[11] Therein, however, danger loomed.

If, in the aftermath of Plataea and Mycale, the Spartans were of two minds, so were the Athenians. Shortly after these battles, Themistocles had come to the conclusion that in the Aegean Persia was a spent force. All that the Athenians had to do was to keep up their fleet and sustain the alliance they were in the process of forging with the islanders. In his estimation, Lacedaemon was now the only remaining substantial threat to Athens—and everything that he did in and after 476 was aimed at weakening Sparta and strengthening Athens's position within Hellas.

Cimon, son of the Miltiades who had led the Athenians to victory against the Persians at Marathon, was of a different opinion. He wanted to shore up Athens's alliance with Sparta and vigorously wage war against Xerxes—ousting the Mede from Thrace, liberating the Greek cities situated on the Anatolian coast, and enriching everyone involved by selling the human beings captured and the other booty collected in the process.

In the debate that took place between these two figures at Athens, Cimon was victorious. His compatriots were eager for revenge against Persia, and they remembered the Spartans most vividly as their comrades in a time of great peril. Themistocles in due course they ostracized. But although, ca. 472, he had to withdraw from Athens for the ten-year term stipulated by the law establishing ostracism as an institution, he remained intent, while abroad, on doing what he could to weaken Lacedaemon.

In consequence, when Themistocles left Athens, he headed for Argos, where enemies of Sparta could expect a warm welcome. From there, Thucydides reports, he traveled about the Peloponnese—where Lacedaemon's Arcadian and Elean allies were with some frequency inclined to rebellion.[12] It can hardly be an accident that it was during his period of enforced exile that the Tegeans and Argives formed an alliance and, in 469, compelled the Lacedaemonians to fight a major battle in the vicinity of Tegea. Nor can it have been fortuitous that, within the army these two communities deployed against Sparta, there were Athenian volunteers in numbers worthy of mention by the poet Simonides. Nor should we be surprised that not long thereafter a Lacedaemonian delegation appeared at Athens acknowledging Pausanias's Medism, reporting that he had been involved in an intrigue with the Helots, and providing evidence suggesting that the victor of Salamis had been party to the regent's plot. The Spartans were quite rightly afraid of the Athenian.

Themistocles was a force of nature. He it was who foresaw Xerxes's invasion and persuaded his compatriots to build a great fleet in anticipation and take to the sea. He also appears to have recognized that there was only one way to defeat Lacedaemon—which was to exploit the resentment and ambitions of the Argives and rally, with their help, Sparta's Peloponnesian allies against their hegemon and, then, foment domestic unrest within Lacedaemon and spark a Helot rebellion within its domain.[13]

At the time that the Lacedaemonians found themselves faced with a hostile coalition of Argives and Tegeans, there was a Persian resurgence; and, ca. 469, the Athenians and their allies in the Delian League, under Cimon's leadership, found themselves forced to fight a great battle on both sea and land on the south coast of Anatolia opposite Cyprus—where the Eurymedon River entered the Mediterranean. Cimon's victory on this occasion was decisive, and Plutarch tells us that it occasioned negotiations with the Mede that produced a settlement of outstanding differences.[14] Had it not been for Xerxes's assassination soon thereafter in 465, the Hellenes' long war with Persia might well have come to an end at this time.

Cimon, who took great care to sustain Athens's alliance with Sparta, is apt to have squared these negotiations with the Lacedaemonians. For them, as for the Athenians, such a settlement would have brought relief. But the supposition that peace was at hand is almost certain to have occasioned anxiety as well. The Spartans accepted Athens's hegemony at sea because it suited their interests to have the Athenians and their allies do their fighting for them. But once such fighting was no longer needed, once the

Persians were out of the picture, the dramatic growth in Athenian power that had produced this achievement cannot have seemed so benign. It was time, many a Lacedaemonian thought, to clip the wings of their uppity ally.

Two things worried the Spartans. The first derived from the fact that Themistocles had brought home to them their vulnerability. The Argives had long been a threat. The Lacedaemonians' allies within the Peloponnese, especially the Arcadians, were more often restive than not; and, without much support at home, this enterprising Athenian had successfully exploited these circumstances and put Lacedaemon in great peril. What, they asked themselves, might Themistocles have accomplished had he enjoyed full support from his compatriots?

Their second source of worry stemmed from the fact that Athens's maritime alliance had evolved into something sinister, which resembled Persia's empire. The cities that joined the Delian League had three options. They could contribute triremes fully manned to the allied fleet; they could supply empty galleys to be crewed by the Athenians or those whom they hired; or they could substitute a contribution in specie that would enable the Athenians to build and themselves man the missing ships. As time went on, fewer and fewer cities contributed triremes, and the navy fully under Athens's control grew in size and strength. Moreover, when cities failed to make the required contribution, the Athenians (with the support of their compliant allies) resorted to force. They did so against free riders, such as Carystos in Euboea, which had refused to join the league. They did so against cities, such as Naxos, that had neglected and then refused to meet their obligations.[15]

The Spartans had reason to fear that this behemoth, which had grown up gradually and unobtrusively on their doorstep, would someday be deployed against their alliance. With the help of Cimon, they had disposed of Themistocles, who had fled from Argos to Corcyra and on to Persia. But the man had a great many admirers at Athens, and someday they would surely come to power. The Lacedaemonians could hardly be content to depend for their security on the vagaries of Athenian politics.

FROM PEACE TO WAR

The Spartans were not alone in reassessing the situation. The Athenians did so as well—as did the other members of their league. While they were at war with Persia, the Athenians had not, as far as we can tell, done anything to take undue advantage of their allies. Once, however, Cimon's brother-in-law Callias had forged with Persia what seemed likely to be a lasting détente, they altered their policy. Thasos, just off the coast of Thrace, was arguably the wealthiest member of the Delian League. The island on which the Thasians resided was rich in gold, marble, lead, copper, and silver; and, in the range of mountains that stretched a few miles inland along the Thracian shore, there were mines, so rich in silver and gold that they had long been considered of great importance. The Thasians controlled the most important of these mines; and, by means of the trading settlements they had founded inland and along the coast, they profited handsomely from the others.

Had the Athenians encroached upon Thasos's continental domain at a time when the Persians were still highly visible as a threat, the latter's citizens might well have acquiesced. When, however, the Athenians did so after forging a peace of sorts with the Mede, the Thasians, who no longer supposed they needed Athens's protection and who had a fleet of their own, launched a rebellion. Then, when Cimon defeated them at sea late in the summer of 465 and in the fall initiated a siege, they dispatched an embassy to Lacedaemon in search of help. From the authorities at Sparta they secured a pledge: in the spring of 464, at the opening of the campaigning season, the Lacedaemonians would rally their allies and launch an invasion of Attica.[16]

Had the Spartans kept their pledge, the Athenians would not have been able to defend their territory. They did not have a hoplite force of sufficient size. Nor were they in a position to withdraw behind their walls and wait for the Peloponnesians to leave. In the years following Xerxes's invasion, remunerative work had become available in the town of Athens and at its port as never before, and the community's population had grown by leaps and bounds. Athenians in large numbers now worked in the city's dockyards, rowed in its fleets, and administered its empire. These Athenians tended to live in or quite near Athens and the Piraeus, and there was no longer room within their walls sufficient to accommodate a great host of fugitives from the countryside. Moreover, although the Piraeus could import food from abroad and withstand a siege, the town of Athens—situated, as it was, some five miles inland from its port—could not hold out for long. Had the forces of the Peloponnesian League invaded Attica, Athens would have had to come to terms—and that might well have required the dismemberment of its empire, or its reconstitution as an alliance of genuinely independent cities presided over by Lacedaemon.

In the event, however, the promised invasion never took place. Sometime in the intervening winter, a series of earthquakes shook Laconia. The epicenter was close to the constituent villages of Lacedaemon. All but five of the Spartans' houses collapsed. Half of the Spartiates were reportedly killed; and, all in all, something on the order of twenty thousand Lacedaemonians lost their lives. Moreover, the earthquake occasioned a Helot rebellion in Laconia that spread to and encompassed the Pamisos valley in Messenia;[17] and to contain it the Lacedaemonians found themselves forced to call in support from their allies—including the Athenians.

In the emergency, Cimon was able to rally his compatriots and lead an army into Laconia, and there the Athenians were joined by the Aeginetans, the Mantineians, the Plataeans, and, we must presume, forces from a great many other communities. A few years later—after the revolt had been contained, the Helots had been defeated in a pitched battle in Messenia, and the remaining rebels had barricaded themselves up on Mount Ithome—the Spartans dispatched a second embassy to Athens with another request. Thanks to their efforts to evict the Persians from their strongholds along the Anatolian coast, the Athenians had ample experience in siege warfare. The Spartans had none. They were adept at hoplite warfare—conducted by infantrymen, bearing heavy, interlocking shields, arrayed in a phalanx eight men deep. If they had any agile, light-armed troops suited to combat on rough ground in mountainous terrain, they were drawn from the Helot population. What they wanted from Athens were specialists—"picked men"—with the requisite experience, and this Cimon managed to produce in the face of fierce opposition from men like Ephialtes and Pericles, who shared the strategic vision projected by Themistocles and longed for Lacedaemon's demise.[18]

The army of specialists that Cimon led to Messenia did not remain there long. Something happened while they were on campaign that undermined Cimon's position at Athens. We know that, in his absence, Ephialtes and Pericles managed to carry out a constitutional reform that eliminated an important source of his political strength and rendered Athens more democratic, and we are told that the "picked men" under his command expressed discontent with the unsavory task they were assigned. Why, they apparently asked, should we assist the Spartans in subjugating our fellow Greeks?

It is not hard to guess what event it was that suddenly undermined Cimon's standing. The siege of Thasos, which he had initiated, is said to have lasted into the third year.[19] There is a good chance that, shortly after Cimon left for Messenia, word reached Athens that the siege had come to an end; and there is reason to suspect that the Athenians also became aware at this time of the pledge that the Lacedaemonians had made to the Thasians. We know that they eventually learned of the pledge, and there is no more likely occasion.

If this is what happened, it explains much more than the sudden collapse of support for Cimon at Athens and the pronounced grumbling among the Athenians deployed in Messenia. The Spartans' awareness of the difficulties in which their Athenian champion found himself and of the reasons for the anger now directed at them may well account for their awkward and transparently disingenuous decision to send Cimon and his specialists back to Athens as supposedly unneeded at a time when their mission remained unaccomplished.[20]

It was after Cimon's return that his compatriots renounced their long-standing connection with Lacedaemon, forged an alliance with the erstwhile Medizers of Thessaly and Argos, and voted at an ostracism to send the proud son of Miltiades abroad for a ten-year term. Soon thereafter, when Corinthian bullying induced the Megarians to turn to the Athenians for protection, the latter seized the opportunity to lure them out of the Spartan alliance.

Megara was a city of great strategic importance. Like its neighbor Corinth, it occupied and commanded the isthmus that connected the Peloponnese with the Greek mainland. If the Athenians could garrison Megara and its ports, Nisaea on the Saronic Gulf and Pegae on the Gulf of Corinth; build walls to link the town of Megara with Nisaea; and rigorously guard the passes through Mount Geraneia on the eastern edge of Megara's domain, they could secure the Megarid, control egress from the Peloponnese, and prevent the Spartans and their allies from invading Attica.[21]

The fact that the Lacedaemonians were themselves not quick to respond to these hostile acts tells us much about the gravity of the difficulties they faced near to home—where, as Thucydides puts it, "they were constrained by wars"—wars in which they had to contend with the Helots on Mount Ithome, the Tegeans and their allies elsewhere within Arcadia, and the Argives.[22] The Spartans' absence from the struggle initiated by Athens did not then and should not now obscure the fact that the Athenians were now, to the best of their abilities, waging war against their erstwhile ally.

THE FIRST ROUND

In the first few years of the struggle that then broke out, while the Spartans were preoccupied, the Athenians acted to consolidate their position. First, they bolstered the Argives, who were in the process of eliminating Mycenae and Tiryns as rivals within the Argolid. Then, they annihilated the fleets deployed by the Aeginetans and the Corinthians and turned the Saronic Gulf into an Athenian lake. All the while they were building what they called Long Walls to link the town of Athens with the Piraeus and Phaleron Bay and turn Athens as a political community into a virtual island—impervious to assault by land and capable of importing food from the entire Mediterranean.[23]

In 458—spurred, we must suspect, by Corinth and their other allies—the Lacedaemonians finally stirred. Under the command of a figure named Nicomedes—who appears to have been regent for his brother Pausanias's underage, royal son Pleistoanax—they shipped across the Gulf of Corinth a hoplite army, composed of 1,500 Spartiates and perioeci and of a great host, ten thousand or more, drawn from among their Peloponnesian allies. Its stated objective was to defend the Spartans' kinsmen in Doris against their Phocian neighbors. But it appears to have also made arrangements at Delphi in Lacedaemon's interest. Moreover, it moved, thereafter, into Boeotia, where it sought to restore the hegemony of Athens's ancient enemy Thebes; and it then marched southeast and presented itself on the borders of Attica at Tanagra—quite near Oropus, Athens's strategically vital port of embarkation for the nearby island of Euboea. In that position, it was about as far as one could get within Boeotia from the road leading back to the Peloponnese.

We are told that the Peloponnesians were invited to intervene in Attica by certain Athenians—wealthy landholders who were unhappy with the new order established by Ephialtes and who opposed the building of the Long Walls and Athens's adoption of a new military strategy founded on a decision not to defend against invasion of the territory farmed by a majority of its citizens. It is hard to believe that Nicomedes's true mission was not, from the outset, focused on this. Once those Long Walls were completed and Athens was made a virtual island, it would be difficult, if not impossible, for the Spartans to rein in, much less subjugate, the

Athenians. This much the Lacedaemonians and their allies surely understood.

In responding to the threat posed by Nicomedes and his army, the Athenians were not behindhand, and they were more than ready. The twenty-five miles to Tanagra they marched with their entire levy, and they brought with them a thousand Argive hoplites and an unknown number from Cleonae, a considerable body of infantrymen from their Aegean allies, and a cavalry force from Thessaly.

They should have been a match for Nicomedes's Peloponnesians. The Athenian army is said to have amounted to fourteen thousand hoplites, and Nicomedes's, to eleven thousand five hundred. If he had some Boeotian support as well, as we are told, it must have come largely from Thebes; and, given what Thucydides reports concerning the makeup of Nicomedes's infantry force, the Theban contribution must have been for the most part composed of cavalry familiar with the Boeotian plain and well-suited to deployment on it—for that is what Nicomedes is almost certain to have sorely lacked.

The battle itself was hard fought, and we are told by late sources that it lasted two days. It was, we must suppose, a classic clash of two long phalanxes made up of heavy infantrymen armed with interlocking shields, thrusting spears, and short swords and variously equipped with metal helmets or caps made of felt and with corselets or cuirasses and greaves made of brass. We must imagine serried ranks of exhausted hoplites stubbornly pushing, shoving, spearing, and stabbing for hours on end in the hot summer sun while the cavalry forces covered their flanks. In such a battle, everything turned on strength and endurance, and that will have been especially true if the conflict actually continued for two days.

On this particular occasion, we are told, there were a great many lives lost on both sides—including three or perhaps even four hundred of the thousand Argives—and, at a crucial juncture, at least a part of the highly disciplined Thessalian cavalry force shamelessly switched sides. When it was all over, the Lacedaemonians and their Peloponnesian allies, though badly battered, still held the field. But they had not achieved that at which they aimed; and, when they withdrew through the Megarid with no further interference on the part of the Athenians, they left the latter free to finish the Long Walls, subdue Aegina, and conquer Boeotia.[24]

In the aftermath, the Athenians bore down on the Spartans and their allies. First, their commander Tolmides with a fleet of fifty triremes circumnavigated the Peloponnese, raiding the territory of the Peloponnesian cities en route, seizing Cythera, burning the docks at the Lacedaemonian port of Gytheum, and wreaking havoc within the Gulf of Corinth.[25] Three years later, when the Spartans came to terms with the rebels on Mount Ithome and the latter were allowed to withdraw from the Peloponnese, Tolmides settled them at Naupactus on the northern shore of the Gulf of Corinth near the mouth of that body of water—where no more than a mile separates northern Greece from the Peloponnese. From there, we can assume, and perhaps also from the Megarian port of Pegae, Athens's triremes instituted a blockade, similar to the one they would initiate in 429, aimed at crippling the economy of Corinth, Lacedaemon's most important ally.[26] Athens's immediate purpose was Sparta's humiliation, which it hoped to achieve by demonstrating Lacedaemon's inability to defend the interests of its allies. Athens's larger aim was to encourage Argos and Tegea and recreate the conditions, conducive to Sparta's defeat on land at the hands of its own allies, that Themistocles had with some success attempted to foster in the late 470s and early 460s.

Given time, this strategy might have worked. But the Athenians did not have the requisite time. In 465, Xerxes had been assassinated by a subordinate unhappy with the settlement he had reached with Athens.[27] In the aftermath, his son and heir Artaxerxes renewed the war in Greece; and, in 460, an Athenian fleet, sent to counter the Persians on Cyprus and in Phoenicia, was diverted to Egypt to support a rebellion against the Great King. Had the Athenians been prudently parsimonious in support of this rebellion, its collapse in the face of a Persian invasion six years later would not have much mattered. But their commitment and that of their allies was immense. Between them, they lost roughly 235 triremes—which is to say, approximately forty-seven thousand men.[28]

This brought Athens's advance in Greece to a sudden halt and occasioned the recall of Cimon, who journeyed to Lacedaemon and persuaded the Spartans that it was in their interest to suspend the war and give Athens five years in which to turn back the inevitable Persian attack. For this, the Athenians paid a steep price. The Argives were left to the mercy of the Spartans and under duress negotiated with them a peace of thirty years' duration; and the Tegeans, when abandoned, succumbed to pressure and reemerged as a narrow oligarchy fiercely loyal to Lacedaemon.[29]

Then, in 446, after the Athenians had annihilated yet another Persian fleet at Cypriot Salamis and after Artaxerxes had agreed to renew the peace that had been fatal to his father,[30] the Spartans engineered a collapse of Athens's position on the Greek mainland. First, in all likelihood at Lacedaemon's instigation, there was a rebellion in Boeotia, which resulted in the ambush and defeat of an Athenian army at Coronea and in Athens's abandonment of its quest to dominate that region. Soon thereafter, as if according to plan, there was a revolt encompassing all of the cities in Euboea, the island nearest Attica and, because of its proximity and size, the one most important to the Athenians. Then, when, as was predictable, Pericles led an army to Euboea, a rebellion broke out in the Megarid resulting in an opening of the passes through Mount Geraneia; the introduction of an army of Corinthians, Sicyonians, and Epidaurians into Megara; and a massacre of that city's Athenian garrison. And finally, when Pericles led his army back from Euboea into the Megarid, there was an invasion of Attica by the Spartans and their Peloponnesian allies. The Athenians were caught flat-footed on this occasion—with at least part of their army isolated behind enemy lines. They could not take full advantage of the security afforded them by their Long Walls, and they had to agree to a peace of thirty years' duration requiring them to jettison the alliances they had made within the Peloponnese and give up their acquisitions therein.[31]

THE SECOND ROUND

The army that intimidated the Athenians in 446 was led by Pleistoanax, the young Agiad king of Lacedaemon. Had he seized on the opportunity afforded him to inflict on Athens a devastating defeat, had he introduced garrisons into the cities in revolt on Euboea and bolstered their claim for independence, the odds are good that there would have been rebellions throughout the Aegean and that the Athenian Empire would have collapsed. If Pleistoanax did nothing of the sort, it was presumably because he did not think Lacedaemon fit for taking on the responsibilities hitherto shouldered by the Athenians and because he was aware that, if there was anarchy in the Aegean, the Persians would wade in. The dilemma that had occasioned Sparta's toleration of the growth in Athens's power had not disappeared.

The Lacedaemonians were nonetheless unhappy with what their king had left undone, and they took it out on him, charging that the young man and his chief adviser had succumbed to bribery, and subsequently driving them into exile. They did not, however, repudiate the arrangements he had made.[32] This was surely in part due to the fact that, in the interim, the Athenians had subdued Euboea and that it would not be easy once again to catch them flat-footed with a substantial number of hoplites outside Attica and in peril. But it was no doubt also in part due to the fact that, given the permanent Helot threat, there were not a great many Lacedaemonians who wanted to take on the monumental task of deterring a Persian invasion—especially since they knew that this might well endanger the Spartan regime and way of life.

Neither side really expected the settlement to last. The so-called Thirty Years' Peace was, after all, a truce of limited duration—and if an opportunity presented itself for gaining a decisive advantage, there were numerous individuals in both cities who were prepared to renew the war on short notice. In 440, for example, when the island of Samos rebelled, the authorities at Lacedaemon were ready and willing to seize the occasion.³³ Moreover, in the mid-430s, when a dispute between Corinth and Corcyra provided Athens with an opportunity for expanding its influence in a region regarded by the Corinthians as essential to their security, the Athenians did not shy away from the attendant risks. Instead, they chose to exploit the conflict with the aim of driving a wedge between Sparta and Corinth. Their purpose was to enrage the Corinthians without technically breaching the agreement with Sparta, and their leader Pericles was persuaded that even if this eventuated in a war, if the Persians remained on the sidelines, as they were by then wont to do, Athens would "win through" by demonstrating Lacedaemon's inability to defeat it; and he was convinced that Athens would then be able to negotiate a peace, destructive to Sparta's prestige, that would result in Corinth's angrily bolting from the Peloponnesian League and taking other cities with it, as it was already, at this time, threatening to do.³⁴

That this did not happen quickly, soon after the outbreak of what modern scholars call the "Peloponnesian War," was a consequence of the demographically devastating plague that struck Athens shortly after the onset of that conflict. But, after faltering briefly, the Athenians stubbornly dug in their heels, and Pericles's expectations were eventually met. Athens's system of fortification, supplemented by a third wall built from the town of Athens to the Piraeus in the interwar period, proved effective. As predicted, the Spartan invasions accomplished nothing. As expected, in and around the Peloponnese, the Athenians did what they had done in the previous war—and eventually, when they fortified a headland in Messenia, introduced into it Messenian troops from Naupactus, and captured a small Spartan force involved in an attempt to dislodge these troops, the Lacedaemonians sued for peace.

Although, in the absence of Pericles, who was killed by the plague, it took repeated setbacks to persuade the Athenians that they should negotiate terms, when they finally did so the

Corinthians did bolt, just as they had threatened—and chaos ensued within the Peloponnese. The Mantineians and Eleans aligned themselves with Argos and a small army of Athenians intervened to support this coalition against the Lacedaemonians. Had the Eleans been present at the Battle of Mantineia in 418 and had the Athenians sent not one but four thousand hoplites, victory in the manner first envisaged by Themistocles would almost certainly have been achieved.[35]

In the aftermath, the Athenians once again did what they had done in Egypt—which was to ignore the risks, send a massive expeditionary force to a distant land on a perilous mission, dispatch substantial reinforcements when trouble developed, and lose all of the ships deployed and nearly all of the men. On this occasion, however, when news of the debacle, this time in Sicily, reached Hellas, the Athenians were shown no mercy—no mercy at all. Darius II, the bastard son and heir of Artaxerxes, offered aid to Lacedaemon through his satraps Tissaphernes and Pharnabazus, and the Spartans and their allies swallowed with difficulty their hostility to the Mede and accepted it. Thereafter, when they experienced setbacks, Tissaphernes or Pharnabazus and, later, Darius's younger son Cyrus came to their rescue; and eventually the Athenians—who were short of money and manpower and inclined to faction-fighting—blundered ignominiously, lost a great battle at sea, and were forced to accept terms that required them to abandon their fleet and their empire and tear down their Long Walls.[36]

AMBIVALENCE AND OVERWEENING AMBITION

This conflict—which was rooted in the deep ambivalence of an ascendant power and in the untrammeled and, at times, extravagant ambition of a rising power—was arguably unavoidable; and victory could have gone to either side. Before the Long Walls were built, the Spartans had the advantage, but they were reluctant to exploit it. They did not want to take on the maritime hegemony themselves, and they feared that the Persians might return. So they acquiesced in the growth of Athenian power. Then, when a settlement seemed to have been reached with Persia and they became less reluctant to exploit their advantage, they were hobbled at a crucial moment by an earthquake and a Helot revolt.

After the Long Walls were built, the Athenians had the advantage. But they squandered it by foolishly overextending themselves in Egypt; and in 446 the Lacedaemonians outwitted and would have eliminated them had they not once again given way to the reluctance that persistently constrained them.

When war resumed, as was inevitable given the peculiar character of each of the two powers, the Athenians once again had the advantage. But the plague got in their way, and when they managed to break up the Peloponnesian League, they failed fully to exploit the opportunity. Then, finally by foolishly mounting an expedition to Sicily and overextending themselves a second time, they imperiled their city, and the Persians and Lacedaemonians formed an uneasy alliance that eventually brought them down.

It is difficult to draw a straightforward moral from what happened in Greece that is applicable to the rivalry now existing between, for example, the United States and China.[37] It is, of course, true that the United States is an ascendant, or hegemonic, power, and China is a rising power; and it is also the case that their rivalry could easily eventuate in armed conflict. But neither modern polity is much like either ancient city. Both are technologically dynamic, commercial societies apt to look on war as, at best, a necessary evil. The ancient Greeks lived in technologically stagnant, martial polities that relished armed conflict and profited from the spoils. In contrast with the United States, Sparta commanded the land, not the sea. In contrast with China, Athens commanded the sea, not the land. Moreover, politically, the United States has more in common with Athens than with Sparta, and China has more in common with Sparta than with Athens. And, perhaps most important of all, the world in which Athens and Sparta came to blows was not bipolar as students of their conflict have long been inclined to suppose.[38] It was tripolar. The Persians were, as the war's outcome suggests, always present—even when observing at a safe distance from offstage. One of the many things that Thucydides has to teach us is that the devil is in the details.

A student of contemporary affairs looking for an instructive analogue pertinent to the current situation, would, I think, do better to study the relations between Germany and Britain in the years leading up to World War I. In that situation two commercial powers squared off—the one an aggressive, authoritarian, newly minted land power on the rise, and the other an old, satiated, liberal sea power that had long been ascendant in the world beyond the continent of Europe. It was when the former took to the sea and threatened the security of the latter that hostility replaced the friendliness that had governed their relations in the past. That is the lesson, offered by history, that statesmen in our day and time should ponder.

RECOMMENDATIONS FOR FURTHER READING

For someone interested in the rivalry that emerged in the fifth century BCE between Sparta and Athens, there is no substitute for reading Thucydides, who charted their relations; and there is no edition in English better than *The Landmark Thucydides*, Robert J. Strassler, ed. (New York: Free Press, 1998), which provides maps, time lines, an excellent introduction, and a set of useful appendices. Those interested in the prehistory of this development should read Herodotus in *The Landmark Herodotus: The Histories*, Robert J. Strassler, ed. (New York: Pantheon, 2007), which has all of the virtues of its predecessor. The last years of the Peloponnesian War are covered by Diodorus Siculus in the thirteenth book of his universal history, which can most conveniently be found in Diodorus Siculus, *The Persian Wars to the Fall of Athens: Books 11–14.34 (480–401 BCE)*, Peter Green, tr. (Austin: University of Texas Press, 2010); as well as in the first two books of Xenophon's *Hellenika*, and here again there is no English edition as good as *The Landmark*

Xenophon's Hellenika, Robert J. Strassler, ed. (New York: Pantheon, 2009).

The classic modern study of the growth of Athenian power is Russell Meiggs, *The Athenian Empire* (Oxford: Clarendon Press, 1972), which needs adjustment in light of what we have learned in the intervening years concerning the dating of certain Athenian inscriptions: see Peter J. Rhodes, "After the Three-Bar *Sigma* Controversy: The History of Athenian Imperialism Reassessed," *Classical Quarterly* n.s. 58, no. 2 (2008): 500–506. The classic scholarly study of the conflict between Sparta and Athens is Donald Kagan's magisterial four-volume *New History of the Peloponnesian War* (Ithaca, NY: Cornell University Press, 1969–1987). His account has recently been challenged in different ways by two of his students: J. E. Lendon, in his *Song of Wrath: The Peloponnesian War Begins* (New York: Basic Books, 2010); and Paul A. Rahe, in *Sparta's First Attic War* (New Haven, CT: Yale University Press, 2019) and *Sparta's Second Attic War* (New Haven, CT: Yale University Press, 2020). For a study of the second round in the Sparta-Athens conflict from a thematic perspective, see Victor Davis Hanson, *A War Like No Other* (New York: Random House, 2011). Regarding the political culture of Athens and the factional strife that broke out within the city in the period beginning with the Sicilian Expedition, see Mark Munn's *The School of History: Athens in the Age of Socrates* (Berkeley: University of California Press, 2000), and Jacob Howland, *Glaucon's Fate* (Philadelphia: Paul Dry Books, 2018).

NOTES

1. Winston S. Churchill, *My Early Life: A Roving Commission* (Glasgow: William Collins Sons, 1959), 235.

2. For a recent overview, see Paul A. Rahe, *The Grand Strategy of Classical Sparta: The Persian Challenge* (New Haven, CT: Yale University Press, 2015), cited hereinafter as *The Persian Challenge*.

3. Opposition to Athens's rebuilding its city walls: Thucydides 1.90.1–2; Diodorus 11.39.1–3; Nepos, *Themistocles* 6.2–4; Plutarch, *Themistocles* 19.1–2. Evidence strongly suggesting (but not proving) Corinthian pres-

sure at this time: Thucydides 1.69.1. Aeginetan role: Plutarch, *Themistocles* 19.2.

4. For the geopolitical situation of Sparta and the manner in which it coped, see Paul A. Rahe, *The Spartan Regime: Its Character, Origins, and Grand Strategy* (New Haven, CT: Yale University Press, 2016).

5. See Rahe, *The Persian Challenge*, 167–80, 208–40.

6. Themistocles at Sparta: Thucydides 1.90.5–91.7; Diodorus 11.40.2–4; Nepos, *Themistocles* 7. Plutarch's contention (*Themistocles* 19.1–3) that he bribed the ephors in charge may well be right. For further details, see Paul A. Rahe, *Sparta's First Attic War: The Grand Strategy of Classical Sparta, 478–446 B.C.* (New Haven, CT: Yale University Press, 2019), 24–33.

7. Consider Thucydides 1.93, 2.13.6–7 with Aristophanes, *Equites* 813–16; Diodorus 11.41–43; Nepos, *Themistocles* 6.1; Plutarch, *Themistocles* 19.3–5 in light of Rahe, *The Persian Challenge*, 76–104 (esp. 92–100).

8. Leotychidas's proposal and its rejection: Herodotus 9.106.2–4; Diodorus 11.37.1–3 with Rahe, *The Persian Challenge*, 324–26, 331–33.

9. Pausanias at Plataea: Rahe, *The Persian Challenge*, 300–323, 333–36. Pausanias at sea: Thucydides 1.94.1–2; Aristotle, *Constitution of the Athenians* 23.4; Diodorus 11.44.1–3; Nepos, *Pausanias* 2.1–2, *Aristides* 2.2. Misconduct and complaints: Herodotus 8.3.2; Thucydides 1.95.1–5 (with 75.2, 96.1); Diodorus 11.44.3–6; Nepos, *Pausanias* 2.2–6, *Aristides* 23.1–5, *Cimon* 6.1–3; Aristodemus 104 F6.2–3, 8.1, in *Die Fragmente der griechischen Historiker* [*FGrH*], ed. Felix Jacoby (Berlin: Weidmann, 1926).

10. Origins of Athenian maritime hegemony: Thucydides 1.96, 3.10.3–4, 5.18.5, 6.76.3–4; Aristotle, *Constitution of the Athenians* 23.4–5; Diodorus, 11.44.6, 47; Nepos, *Aristides* 2.3; Plutarch, *Aristides* 25.1–3; Aristodemus, *FGrH* 104 F7 with Russell Meiggs, *The Athenian Empire* (Oxford: Clarendon Press, 1972), 42–67, 459–64.

11. Pausanias suspected as Medizer: Thucydides 1.95.1–5, 128.3–131.1; Diodorus 11.44.3–6; Nepos, *Pausanias* 2.2–6; Plutarch, *Cimon* 6.1–3; Aristodemus, *FGrH* 104 F6.2–3. Leotychidas caught with bribe: Herodotus 6.72; Pausanias 3.7.8–10; Plutarch, *Moralia* 859d. Evidence for Spartan ambivalence: Thucydides 1.92; Plutarch, *Themistocles* 19.3; Diodorus 11.50. Maritime war left to Athens: Diodorus 11.50 and Plutarch, *Aristides* 23.7 with Donald Kagan, *The Outbreak of the Peloponnesian War* (Ithaca, NY: Cornell University Press, 1969), 51–52, 378–79.

12. Themistocles's travels in the Peloponnese: Thucydides 1.135.3. Circumstances promising. Antony Andrewes, "Sparta and Arcadia in the Early Fifth Century," *Phoenix* 6, no. 1 (1952): 1–5. Cf. W. G. Forrest, "Themistokles and Argos," *Classical Quarterly* n.s. 10, no. 3–4 (1960): 221–41, with James L. O'Neil, "The Exile of Themistokles and Democracy in the Peloponnese,"

Classical Quarterly n.s. 31, no. 2 (1981): 335–46, who provides a partial corrective, and see W. G. Forrest, "Pausanias and Themistokles Again," *Lakōnikaí Spoudaí* 2 (1975): 115–20, and Rahe, *Sparta's First Attic War*, 61–73, 94–105.

13. For a full citation and discussion of the scattered ancient evidence pertinent to these developments and of much of the modern scholarship, see Rahe, *Sparta's First Attic War*, 53–115.

14. Victory at Eurymedon: Thucydides 1.100.1; Plutarch, *Cimon* 12.5–13.3. Peace negotiations thereafter: Plutarch, *Cimon* 13.4–5 with Ernst Badian, "The Peace of Kallias," in *From Plataea to Potidaea: Studies in the History and Historiography of the Pentecontaetia*, ed. Ernst Badian (Baltimore, MD: Johns Hopkins University Press, 1993), 1–72, whose controversial argument for accepting Plutarch's testimony I defend in *Sparta's First Attic War*, 83–89.

15. See Meiggs, *The Athenian Empire*, 1–91.

16. Resources of Thasos: Herodotus 6.28.1, 46.2–47.2. Empória: Herodotus 7.109.2, 118; Thucydides 1.100.2; Pseudo-Scylax 67. Encroachment, rebellion, appeal to Lacedaemon, and pledge: Thucydides 1.100.2–101.2; Nepos, *Cimon* 2.5; Diodorus 11.70.1; Plutarch, *Cimon* 14.2.

17. Earthquake and aftershocks: Thucydides 1.101.2, 128.1, 2.27.2, 3.54.5, 4.56.2. Date: Pausanias 4.24.5–6; Plutarch, *Cimon* 16.4. Cf. Diodorus 11.63.1 and Scholia on Aristophanes, *Lysistrata* 1144, which date the earthquake and the attendant revolt to 469/8, with David M. Lewis, "Chronological Notes," in *Cambridge Ancient History*, 2nd ed. (Cambridge: Cambridge University Press, 1992), 5:499–500, who makes sense of their error. Five houses left standing: Plutarch, *Cimon* 16.4–5; Cicero, *De Divinatione* 1.112; Pliny, *Naturalis Historia* 2.191; Aelian, *Varia Historia* 6.7; Polyaenus, *Stratagems* 1.41.3. Twenty thousand Lacedaemonians dead with more than half of all the Spartiates killed: Diodorus 11.63.1–3, 15.66.4. Helot revolt: Thucydides 1.101.2, 2.27.2, 3.54.5, 4.56.2; Critias, ap. Libanius, *Orations* 25.63; Diodorus 11.63.4–64.1; Plutarch, *Cimon* 16.6–7; Pausanias 1.29.8, 3.11.8, 4.24.5–6. Battles and losses: Herodotus 9.33–35, 64.2. See also Plutarch, *Lycurgus* 28.12. For the impact on Lacedaemon, see Timothy Doran, *Spartan Oliganthropia* (Leiden: Brill, 2018).

18. General appeal to allies: Diodorus 11.64.2. Aeginetans, Plataeans, and Mantineians respond: Thucydides 2.27.2, 3.54.8, 4.56.2; Xenophon, *Hellenika* 5.2.3. Athens also: Thucydides 1.102.1–2; Xenophon, *Hellenika* 6.5.33; Diodorus 11.64.2; Plutarch, *Cimon* 16.8–10; Pausanias 1.29.8, 4.24.5–6; Justin, *Epitome* 3.6.2. See Ion of Chios F107 (Leurini) = *FGrH* 392 F14 ap. Plutarch, *Cimon* 16.8 with Aristophanes, *Lysistrata* 1137–44. Appropriateness disputed: Plutarch, *Cimon* 16.9–10. Second appeal to the Athenians during the siege of Ithome: Thucydides 1.102.1–2. Specialists—"select men"—sent: Pausanias 1.29.8.

19. Third year: Thucydides 1.101.3.

20. Surrender of Thasos: Thucydides 1.101.3. Ephialtic reform at Athens: consider Aristotle, *Constitution of the Athenians* 3.6, 8.4, 25, 35.2, 41.2, 43.4, 45.2–3, 47.1, 48.2–5, 49.5, 54.2, 55.2–4; Aristotle, *Politics* 1274a7–8; Philochoros, *FGrH* 326 F64; Plutarch, *Solon* 19.2, *Cimon* 15.2–3, *Pericles* 9.5, 10.7–8, *Moralia* 805d, 812d. Spartans nervous, fear Athenian defection to the Messenians, send Cimon and his soldiers home: Thucydides 1.102.3; Diodorus 11.64.2; Plutarch, *Cimon* 17.3; Pausanias 1.29.8–9, 4.24.6–7; Justin, *Epitome* 3.6.3. On the connection between the Spartan pledge to the Thasians and the breach initiated by the Athenians, see Rahe, *Sparta's First Attic War*, 89–93, 117–45.

21. Renunciation of their Spartan connection, alliance with Argos and Thessaly: Thucydides 1.102.4; Pausanias 1.29.8–9, 4.24.7. Note Thucydides 2.22.3. Cimon ostracized: Plato, *Gorgias* 516d; Nepos, *Cimon* 3.1. Occasion for ostracism: Plutarch, *Cimon* 15.3, 17.3, *Pericles* 9.5. Alliance with Megara: Thucydides 1.103.4; Diodorus 11.79.1–2, read in light of Plutarch, *Cimon* 17.1–2. Import of Mount Geraneia: Thucydides 4.72.1, read in light of 1.107.3.

22. Constrained: Thucydides 1.118.2.

23. For the details, see Rahe, *Sparta's First Attic War*, 145–55, 159–62.

24. Nicomedes's campaign in Doris: Thucydides 1.107.2. See also Diodorus 11.79.4–6, who rightly recognizes in Thucydides's phrase "the Lacedaemonians and the allies" the standard formula for Sparta's Peloponnesian alliance. Delphi: Plutarch, *Cimon* 17.4. Sponsorship of Thebes: Diodorus 11.81.2–3; Justin, *Epitome* 3.6.10 with Plato, *Menexenus* 242a–b. Athenian focus: Ian M. Plant, "The Battle of Tanagra: A Spartan Initiative?" *Historia* 43, no. 3 (1994): 259–74. Battle of Tanagra: Thucydides 1.107.5–108.2 with Herodotus 9.33–35; Plato, *Menexenus* 242a–b; Diodorus 11.80; Plutarch, *Cimon* 17.4–7, *Pericles* 10.1–3; Pausanias 1.29.6–9; and Justin, *Epitome* 3.6.10 as well as Pausanias 5.10.4; *A Selection of Greek Historical Inscriptions to the End of the Fifth Century BC*, ed. Russell Meigs and David Lewis (Oxford: Oxford University Press, 1989) [*ML*], no. 35 = *Inscriptiones graecae* [*IG*], vol. 1, 3rd ed. (Berlin: Berlin-Brandenburg Academy, 1981, 1994), no. 1149 = R. Osborne and P. J. Rhodes, ed. and trans., *Greek Historical Inscriptions 478–404 BC* (Oxford: Oxford University Press, 2017) [*O&R*], no. 111; *ML* no. 36 = *O&R* no. 112; *Supplementum epigraphicae Graecum* [*SEG*], vol. 17 (Leiden: Brill, 1960), 243 = *O&R* no. 117A; and *SEG* vol. 34, 560 = *O&R* no. 117B. Cf. Aristodemus, *FGrH* 104 F12.1. Some Boeotians fight alongside the Lacedaemonians at Tanagra: Plato, *Alcibiades* 1, 112c; Pausanias 1.29.6, 9. Aftermath: Thucydides 1.108.2–4; Diodorus 11.83.1–4. For Sparta, strategic defeat: Plato, *Menexenus* 242a–b.

25. Circumnavigation: Thucydides 1.108.5; Diodorus 11.84.2–8; Pausanias 1.27.5, 4.24.7; Polyaenus, *Stratagems* 3.3.1; Aristodemus, *FGrH* 104 F15.1; Scholia on Aeschines 2.75 (Blass = 78 Dinsdorf).

26. Messenians at Naupactus: Thucydides 1.103.1–3. Point of blockade in 429: Thucydides 2.69.1.

27. Motive for Xerxes's assassination: Justin, *Epitome* 3.1.1–2; Aelian, *Varia Historia* 13.3.

28. For a fuller discussion and citation of the evidence and of the secondary literature than is possible here, see Rahe, *Sparta's First Attic War*, 155–59, 178–86.

29. Recall of Cimon: Plutarch, *Cimon* 17.8 with *Pericles* 10.5, *Moralia* 812f; Athenaeus 13.589e–f. Five-year truce: Thucydides 1.112.1. Argos makes peace with Sparta: Thucydides 5.14.4, 28.2. Tegea subdued: Polyaenus, *Stratagems* 2.10.3.

30. Cypriot Salamis: Thucydides 1.112.2–4; Diodorus 12.3.1–4.6; Nepos, *Cimon* 3.4; Plutarch, *Cimon* 18.1–19.2 (with Phanodemos, *FGrH* 325 F23), *Pericles* 10.4–5; Aristides, *Panathenaic Oration* 151f; *Suda* s. v. *Kímōn*. Epigram: Diodorus 11.62.3 (where the reference to Cyprus shows that the battle in question was not the one fought at Eurymedon, as Diodorus supposes, but the struggle that took place nearly two decades thereafter at Cypriot Salamis). Peace with Artaxerxes: Diodorus 12.4.4 (with 9.10.5 and 15.28). Callias as Athenian interlocutor: Diodorus 12.4.4; Pausanias 1.8.2; Aristodemus, *FGrH* 104 F13; *Suda* s. v. *Kallías*. Terms of agreement: Diodorus 12.4.4–6; Isocrates 4.118–20, 7.80, 12.59; Demosthenes 19.273; Lycurgus, *Against Leocrates* 73; Plutarch, *Cimon* 13.4; Aristides, *Panathenaic Oration* 153; Aristodemus, *FGrH* 104 F13; *Suda* s. v. *Kímōn*. Timetable: Meiggs, *The Athenian Empire*, 124–55, 456–57, 515–18.

31. Coronea: Thucydides 1.113 (with the scholia), 3.62.4, 4.92.6; Diodorus 12.6 (where there is confusion concerning the order of events); Plutarch, *Pericles* 18.2–3, *Comparison of Pericles and Fabius Maximus* 3.3; Aristodemus, *FGrH* 104 F14.2. Euboean and Megarian revolts: Thucydides 1.114.1–2. Megarian revolt and Athenian invasion: Diodorus 12.5.2, confirmed by *IG* I³ 1353. Pleistoanax's appearance, withdrawal, Pericles's reconquest of Euboea, the Thirty Years' Peace: Thucydides 1.114.2–115.1. Note 4.21.3. See Meiggs, *The Athenian Empire*, 181–82.

32. Fate of Pleistoanax and Cleandridas: Thucydides 2.21.1, 5.16.3; Ephorus, *FGrH* 70 F193; Plutarch, *Nicias* 28.4; Diodorus 13.106.10; Antiochus, *FGrH* 555 F 11–12; Polyaenus, *Stratagems* 2.10.1–2, 4–5; Scholia on Aristophanes, *Nubes* 858–59; *Suda* s. v. *déon*. Reasons for fury: Jon E. Lendon, *Song of Wrath: The Peloponnesian War Begins* (New York: Basic Books, 2010), 79–82.

Terms of peace: Thucydides 1.35.2, 40, 44.1, 45.3, 67.2–4, 78.4, 85.2, 140.2, 141.1, 144.2, 145, 7.18; Diodorus 12.7; Pausanias 5.23.4.

33. Spartans propose war at meeting of alliance: Thucydides 1.40.5–6, 41.2, 43.1 with Arnold Hugh Martin Jones, "Two Synods of the Delian and Peloponnesian Leagues," *Proceedings of the Cambridge Philological Society* n.s. 182, no. 2 (1952–1953): 43–46.

34. See Paul A. Rahe, *Sparta's Second Attic War: The Grand Strategy of Classical Sparta, 446–418 B.C.* (New Haven, CT: Yale University Press, 2020), 50–82.

35. See Rahe, *Sparta's Second Attic War*, 83–293.

36. Thucydides 6–8; Xenophon, *Hellenika* 1.1.1–2.2.22; and Diodorus 13.36–107 with Donald Kagan, *The Fall of the Athenian Empire* (Ithaca, NY: Cornell University Press, 1987).

37. Cf. Graham Allison, *Destined for War: Can America and China Escape Thucydides's Trap?* (New York: Houghton Mifflin Harcourt, 2017).

38. Cf. Peter Fliess, *Thucydides and the Politics of Bipolarity* (Baton Rouge: Louisiana State University Press, 1966).

2

THE PUNIC WARS

Barry Strauss

Rome and Carthage fought three wars during the 115-year period from 264 to 149 BCE. They are the First Punic War (264–241), the Second Punic War (218–201), and the Third Punic War (149–146). We call them "Punic" from the Latin *Poenus* or Phoenician, a reference to the foundation of Carthage by Phoenician colonists from Tyre (today in Lebanon) and to the Phoenician language spoken in Carthage. It would be more accurate to call them the Punic-Latin Wars or, better yet, the Roman-Carthaginian Wars.

Collectively they represent a struggle for hegemony between two great powers that ultimately turned into a war of annihilation, ending with the total destruction of one of the two states. At stake in the first war was control of Sicily. The second war escalated from a contest over the future of Carthage's empire in southern Spain to a battle over the continuation of Rome's confederation in Italy and Carthage's alliance system in North Africa. It was a struggle for both to retain great-power status. The third war was the final war of annihilation; if it was not exactly genocide—an attempt to wipe out a people—then certainly it was an exercise in abolishing a state and its elite culture without any prospect of ever coming back.

SOURCES

Historians of the ancient world distinguish between literary sources and sources based in material culture. Literary sources

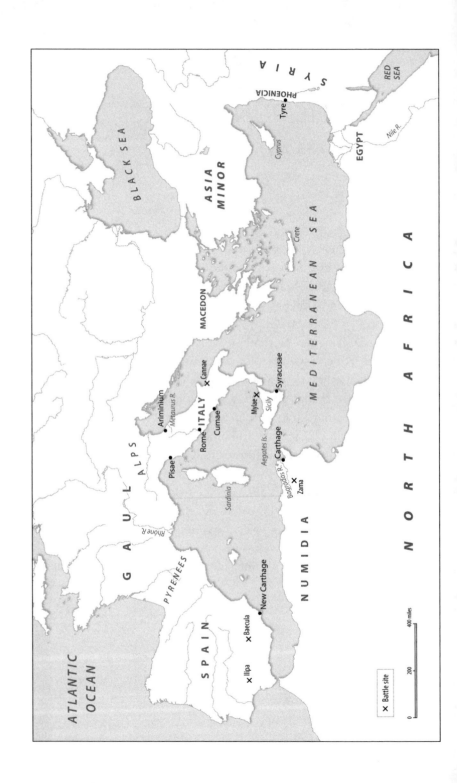

ATLANTIC
OCEAN

GAUL

ALPS

PYRENEES

SPAIN

× Ilipa

× Baecula

New Carthage

NUMIDIA

Rhone R.

Sardinia

Pisae

Rome

Cumae

ITALY

Ariminium

Metaurus R.

× Cannae

Mylae ×

Sicily

Syracusae

Aegates Is.

Bagrados R.

Carthage

×
Zama

MACEDON

Crete

MEDITERRANEAN SEA

NORTH AFRICA

BLACK SEA

ASIA
MINOR

Cyprus

SYRIA

PHOENICIA

Tyre

EGYPT

Nile R.

RED
SEA

× Battle site

0   200   400 miles

are the formal writings of educated, elite authors. Material-cultural sources include the artifacts of art (sculpture, painting, mosaics, etc.), architecture, coins, inscriptions, arms and armor, ships or parts of ships such as rams (particularly as discovered in shipwrecks), roads, and the objects of everyday life (especially pottery). Most of this material has been discovered by archaeologists. It includes the results of surface surveys as well as of excavations. There are also the results of topography, that is, the study of ancient battlefields, roads, and routes. Or rather, one should say, the attempt to reconstruct them. We can almost never pinpoint the site of ancient battles in the field, and the effort to retrace ancient routes (most famously, Hannibal's route over the Alps) is anything but easy, yet the attempt has produced ingenious scholarship.

The archaeological evidence for the Punic Wars is relatively limited. It ranges from coins and a small number of inscriptions to warship rams from the Battle of the Aegates Islands (241 BCE), the last naval battle of the First Punic War, and to arrowheads and catapult balls from the Roman assault that were found in the ruins of Carthage.[1]

Not a single literary source for the Wars survives that was written in Punic, which is primarily a reflection of the destruction of Carthage and its libraries by the Romans. Nor do the earliest Roman histories of the Punic Wars survive. These included, among others, Rome's first history whatsoever, written by Fabius Pictor, a Roman noble and senator who lived during the Second Punic War. He wrote in Greek because that was the language of learning at the time. A century later the Roman L. Coelius Antipater, an erudite scholar of the late second century BCE who wrote in Latin, penned a detailed account of the Second Punic War.

Fortunately, several other literary sources about the Punic Wars in Greek or Latin have been preserved in greater detail. The emphasis in these sources, regardless of their language, is on the Roman point of view, although several of them do at least give some idea of the Carthaginian outlook.

The best and most important surviving source for the wars is a Greek who became a hostage in Rome, Polybius (ca. 200–ca. 120 BCE). A teenager when Hannibal died, Polybius devoted himself to getting accurate information about the wars that made Rome master of the Mediterranean. He is accurate, precise, and a brilliant analyst who made an important contribution to political philosophy as well as to historiography.

The second-best source is Livy (59 BCE–17 CE), who wrote in Latin a history of Rome *ab urbe condita*, "from the foundation of the city." Livy produced his work during the last few decades of the first century BCE, so about 125 years after the end of the Punic Wars. His writing is detailed and gripping but the specifics are often embroidered and the bias is most definitely in favor of Rome. Livy's account of the Second Punic War survives in its entirety. We get glimpses of his narrative of the other two wars from short summaries of most of the 142 chapters (usually called "books") of his work and from the book in Latin of the second century CE Roman writer Florus.

Appian, a Roman citizen and administrator who lived in Rome, was originally a Greek speaker from Alexandria (he died in the 160s). He wrote in Greek a history of Rome through the early second century CE. His coverage of the Punic Wars is uneven, but he provides our sole comprehensive and continuous narrative of the Third Punic War.

Various other authors in the Late Roman Republic or Roman Empire also provide information about the Punic Wars. The most important are Plutarch (50–120), who left us stories of the lives of the Roman leaders Fabius Maximus, Marcellus, and Cato the Elder; and Dio Cassius (mid-160s–ca. 235), who wrote a voluminous history of Rome that included the Punic Wars. We have large summaries of the sections on the Punic Wars, and they are embellishments based in large part on Livy.

To sum up, by far the best literary source overall is Polybius, who is also the most important literary source for the First Punic War. Livy is the most important literary source for the Second Punic War, Appian for the Third Punic War.

FACTORS EXPLAINING THE ORIGIN AND CAUSES
OF THE CONFLICT

At first, Carthage and Rome had separate interests. Carthage was primarily a sea power, Rome primarily a land power. Founded in the late ninth century BCE by Phoenicians from Tyre, Carthage went on to become a great city and acquired a maritime empire. Carthage expanded in the islands and coastal harbors of the central and western Mediterranean, from Sicily to Atlantic Spain. After scattered early settlements, Rome became a city in the eighth century BCE. Afterward, Rome expanded on the Italian peninsula. Between about 509 and 265 BCE, Rome became the ruler of all Italy south of a line running from the Arno to the Rubicon Rivers, that is, from the Tyrrhenian Sea at Pisae (modern Pisa) eastward to Ariminium (modern Rimini) on the Adriatic, leaving only the Po valley and the Alpine foothills independent. Rome conquered those areas as well in the 220s BCE. Roman Italy was built piecemeal and consisted of a combination of Roman territory and colonies, close allies who spoke Latin like the Romans, and other, more diverse cities and territories speaking such languages as Etruscan, Oscan, and Greek.

By the mid-third century BCE, Rome and Carthage were both great powers. A series of treaties between 509 and 279 kept each state to its own sphere, but conflict loomed. When Rome conquered southern Italy (265) only a narrow body of water, the Strait of Messina, separated it from Sicily, then a wealthy and grain-rich prize. Carthage, meanwhile, had failed to conquer eastern Sicily, despite centuries of trying, and remained in the western part of the island. Then in 264 Carthage gained a foothold in the eastern Sicilian city of Messana (modern Messina). Rome decided to intervene.

The competition between Rome and Carthage was primarily a matter of security, although economic motives and personal ambitions also played a part. Ancient Sicily was a wealthy breadbasket, not the region of poverty it has sometimes been in more recent times. Rome could not abide a formidable power like Carthage gaining control of a port on the Strait of Messina, from which it could block the commerce of Rome's allies, the Greek cities of southern Italy. For its part, Carthage could not tolerate the Roman giant's entrance into Sicily. Besides, the prospect of loot and glory loomed large on both sides. That meant war.

SOCIAL, CULTURAL, POLITICAL, ORGANIZATIONAL, AND TECHNOLOGICAL DIMENSIONS

Social, Cultural, and Political Dimensions

The Punic Wars reflect the culture of two aggressive and ambitious military powers living in close proximity in a world in which peace seemed as dishonorable as it was unprofitable. It would have been surprising had the two titans not gone to war.

The two states were, in many ways, mirror images. Rome and Carthage were each mixed regimes, each an oligarchy that now dominated, now struggled with its masses. Each state was controlled by a group of wealthy planters who, in spite of an agrarian ethos, owed a large part of their fortune to commerce. The Carthaginian elite was more mercantile and maritime in its outlook than its Roman counterpart, but it was more agrarian than is often thought. Carthaginian ships traveled as far as West Africa and Ireland, while at home in North Africa, Carthage pioneered the organization of large-scale, single-crop plantations worked by slaves. While some Carthaginian elites wanted to expand abroad, others were satisfied with their domestic holdings.

Carthage was more sophisticated and cosmopolitan than Rome, but then again, Carthage enjoyed a magnificent harbor. Although Italy is a peninsula, it lacks ports. Rome, which had only a mediocre natural harbor nearby, tended to look inward. (In later centuries the emperors engaged in massive, slave-labor-staffed public works projects to carve out an artificial port for the city.) Like many conservative agricultural peoples, Romans tended to be landlubbers. While Rome had only a small navy, Carthage had a

major fleet. It dominated trade in the western Mediterranean and
played a major role in the east. Still, much of Rome's landowning
elite profited from overseas trade.

Each state had access to a considerable treasury and a sizable
population of potential soldiers. Note, though, that Rome used
citizen-soldiers while Carthage did not. If that made Rome more
careful about sending armies abroad, it also rendered Carthage
less concerned about the outcome of its foreign expeditions. Carthage gave its commanders carte blanche but not much support
from home. In the First Punic War in particular, Carthage made
liberal use of mercenaries whose loyalty could not be taken for
granted. Carthage preferred to rely on allies in the Second Punic
War but they were more diverse and polyglot than Rome's allies,
comprising as they did North Africans, Iberians, and northern
Italian Celts as well as a smaller number of Celts from north of the
Alps. A Carthaginian commander had to be a diplomat in order to
hold his multiethnic force together.

Another big difference was in the treatment of allies. Both countries did well at managing them, but Rome did far better. Carthage punished revolts brutally. So did Rome, which projected its
power across the Italian peninsula by planting a series of colonies
and by building the famous Roman roads. But Rome was much
shrewder than Carthage in wielding the carrot as well as the stick.
Rome, for example, secured the allegiance of much of Italy's elite
by granting such privileges as the right to do business in Rome
and to intermarry with Romans. But the greatest privilege of all,
and the most forward-looking Roman policy, was to grant Roman
citizenship—a boon it offered to a large part of the conquered
elite. By 225 BCE, Rome's citizenry consisted of one million free
people, including three hundred thousand adult males subject
to military service. Rome also had access to about 450,000 allied
troops, for a total of 750,000 soldiers. This was a huge number by
ancient standards. While similar statistics for Carthage do not survive, it is clear that its reliable manpower pool was much smaller.

Rome's core allies, the ones bound by the closest and longest-
lasting ties, and so the most loyal and dependable allies, were in

central Italy. They represented a big, reliable pool of soldiers. Carthage preferred the stick and had less dependable allies as a result. Rome proved to be exceptionally good at alliance management. The Carthaginian general Hannibal understood this and he made an extraordinary effort to win his country new allies in the Second Punic War, but he ultimately granted them too many concessions. As a result, the new allies did little to help Carthage. Only Rome seemed to have the recipe that made the core of its allies love it, fear it, and serve it.

As far as we can tell from our limited sources, the Romans also did better at managing civil-military relations. Although Rome watched its generals warily, Carthage was even more chary. The Carthaginian government sometimes punished defeated generals with crucifixion. It is tricky to reconstruct Carthaginian domestic politics since we depend on foreign and largely hostile Greco-Roman sources. But if those sources are right there was a conflict of interest in Carthage between, on the one hand, a group of landed gentry whose focus was on domestic agriculture and trade and, on the other, a warrior elite that looked to conquest and empire abroad. This warrior group often turned to the people rather than to the oligarchical Council of Elders for political support. Although a similar dichotomy existed in Rome, it was possibly more pronounced in Carthage. That might explain both why the Carthaginian government handled its generals so roughly and why it was so grudging about reinforcements and supplies.

Two Ways of War

What the Carthaginians lacked in quantity they made up for in quality. They fostered leadership, innovation, and a knack for doing more with less. It took a long time before the Romans had field commanders who could match the tactical élan of Carthage's best generals, Hamilcar Barca (d. 229 BCE) and his son Hannibal (ca. 246–183 BCE). But élan works best in short, sharp bursts. The Carthaginian way of war succeeded in a quick campaign; it was not suited for a war of attrition against a politically cohesive republic equipped with enormous manpower resources, a firm alliance system, and sage leadership. The Second Punic War saw a gap between two ways of war. Hannibal had a small but lethal professional and polyglot army encamped in enemy territory with little support from Carthage. Rome boasted massive allied forces working from their home base and with seemingly all the time and patience in the world. Hannibal was absorbed with surviving a war of attrition while Rome only got stronger.

For all their similarities, neither Romans nor Carthaginians understood the other fully. Since they tended to be regimented and community-minded themselves, the Romans could not imagine the emergence of an individual genius like Hannibal.

As for Carthage, it seems to have had a wealth of clever people—a group that tends to underestimate the opposition. How easy to caricature the Romans as dull and unimaginative! In fact, they were pragmatic and ruthless. Beneath a veneer of conservatism, Rome embraced change. It proved willing to ditch cherished modes of behavior in order to survive. True, Carthage changed as well, but it found itself flummoxed by an enemy that discovered how to combine suppleness with seemingly inexhaustible manpower resources.

It would be easy to write victor's history from the Roman point of view, but Rome barely avoided defeat in the First Punic War. It might have lost the Second Punic War had Carthage adjusted its strategy after its initial battlefield successes or had no Roman military genius eventually emerged to put Carthage on the defensive. For centuries after the Punic Wars, even when an independent Carthage was long gone, the Romans frightened their children with the phrase *"Hannibal ad portas!"*—"Hannibal is coming to the gates!" Given the beating that Hannibal gave to Rome in the Second Punic War, the fear is understandable.

Technology

Rome won the First Punic War because of its ability to master a new technology: the navy. The most famous weapon in the Second

Punic War was the elephant, but the most strategic was the light cavalryman. In the Third Punic War, Carthage made the most of its wealth and its pluck, but ultimately it was no contest. Rome's military might was so great by this point that the defeat of Carthage was unavoidable. Given the rules of ancient warfare, once it decided to resist the Roman siege to the end, the destruction of the city, the death of much of its population, and the enslavement of the rest were also grim inevitabilities.

When it came to naval warfare Rome showed itself to be flexible if not always elegant. The Romans quickly realized during the First Punic War that, Sicily being an island, they could not prevail unless they could defeat Carthage at sea. Over the space of a generation, Rome turned itself into a competitive sea power. It required the help of its Greek allies in southern Italy and an enormous sacrifice in blood and treasure by the Roman people. Meanwhile, Carthage became a brilliant land power that excelled in seaborne attacks on southern Italy led by a military star, Hamilcar Barca. His arrival in Sicily in 247 rejuvenated the Carthaginian war effort. It was not enough, however, to beat the Roman navy.

At great expense, Rome built a series of large fleets. Carthaginian rowers and helmsmen were well trained and could engage in dazzling maneuvers. The Romans could not compete with that— and so they developed the *corvus*, literally "raven," a grapnel or, more precisely, a hooked metal gangplank that allowed them to send marines onto the enemy's ships. The result was to turn sea battles into land battles, a realm where Roman soldiers held the advantage. Unfortunately, the heavy corvus put Roman ships at greater risk of sinking in storms. Eventually, Roman sailors mastered maneuver warfare and so the navy was able to dispense with the corvus.

Hamilcar did not fight any set, or conventional, battles but relied, rather, on unconventional land tactics and seaborne raids. He kept the Romans on the defensive in western Sicily and caused them major casualties. Meanwhile, he raided both eastern Sicily and the coast of Italy as far north as Cumae, only about 150 miles from Rome. He proved stubbornly impervious to all Roman attempts to defeat and dislodge him.

Hamilcar's successes only underscored the need for the Romans to expand their war aims: in addition to driving Carthage out of Sicily, they wanted to prevent it from being able to project its power into Italy. Hence the need to destroy Carthage's fleet—physically by crushing it in battle, financially by imposing a crippling indemnity, and geographically by forcing Carthage to leave Sicily and all the other islands of the central Mediterranean. But how was Rome to achieve these goals against Hamilcar Barca?

Polybius argues convincingly that the First Punic War was won at sea. His Romans learned a hard lesson: they thought they could win the war by their army alone, but that turned out to be untrue. Polybius wrote:

> For the last five years [247–242] indeed they had entirely abandoned the sea, partly because of the disasters they had sustained there, and partly because they felt confident of deciding the war by means of their land forces; but they now determined for the third time to make trial of their fortune in naval warfare. They saw that their operations were not succeeding according to their calculations, mainly owing to the obstinate gallantry of the Carthaginian general [that is, Hamilcar Barca]. They therefore adopted this resolution from a conviction that by this means alone, if their design were but well directed, would they be able to bring the war to a successful conclusion.[2]

And so, although their treasury was exhausted by the long war, the Romans built one more fleet, financed by a small group of wealthy private citizens. The Carthaginian state was out of money as well, but no private financiers stepped forward there. Rome's new fleet surprised the Carthaginians. The Roman elite assigned a higher priority to winning the competition than did their opposite number in Carthage, and that made all the difference.

The Romans won a great naval victory at the Aegates Islands (known as the Egadi Islands in modern times) off western Sicily in 241. This was the end of the First Punic War. The Carthaginians had to admit defeat and sue for peace. Rome imposed a harsh settlement that drove Carthage from Sicily and crippled it financially to the point where it couldn't pay its mercenaries, who rose in a revolt in North Africa that took a bloody effort before it was suppressed. Meanwhile, Rome treacherously seized Sardinia, another Carthaginian possession. Although this move convinced Carthage that Rome couldn't be trusted, it also denied Carthage a necessary stopping point on the sea route to Italy. Carthage lost its naval edge—permanently, as it turned out. Rome now became the leading naval power of the Mediterranean. Although Carthage eventually built a new fleet, this new fleet could no longer compete with the Roman navy, either in numbers or seamanship.

Nonetheless, the African city found a way to compete against Rome—by building a new empire in southern Iberia. Under the leadership of Hamilcar Barca and his son-in-law and sons, Carthage acquired an area rich in iron and silver and in military manpower. The Romans noticed and they tried to intimidate Carthage, but Hamilcar's eventual successor, his son, the brilliant general Hannibal, refused to be cowed. And so the Second Punic War began.

Hannibal stunned Rome at the outset by marching nine hundred miles overland, with his army, crossing the Alps, and reaching Italy. He brought with him thirty-seven elephants, who survived the mountain snow. They are the most famous weapon of the Punic Wars, but in fact elephants played a relatively small role in the fighting. They served more as a symbol and a terror weapon than as an effective battlefield factor. They were more important as a propaganda image on Hannibal's coins (and in the retelling by frightened Romans) than they were in real life. Hannibal's true key weapon was his army.

Hannibal was a superb tactician. He was a brilliant and inspiring leader of men. He was cunning, unpredictable, and cold-blooded. He was a master of battlefield maneuvers. His specialty was a combined infantry-cavalry attack. No unit was as important as the superb cavalry of Numidia (roughly, modern Algeria).

They were light infantry who could ride around the enemy with terrifying speed and take him in the flank or rear. They played a major role in the defeats that Hannibal inflicted on the Romans again and again in Italy between 218 and 216.

The Romans, by comparison, were unimaginative and unsurprising. They had little taste for cavalry, which they relied largely on their allies to supply. The Romans were infantrymen above all, and they usually deployed their men in a simple, straightforward attack. They won because of their toughness, their manpower, and their wise use of reserves. In the long term, Rome's manpower might wear Hannibal down, but in the short term, it was not enough to outdo him on the battlefield.

Carthage was now Rome's superior in land battle. Unfortunately, the land battles of 218–216 proved to be a hollow victory. Rome reacted to its terrible losses with equanimity. This was a tribute to the leadership provided by the Senate and to the fortitude of the people, but it also reflected Hannibal's limitations. Although he spent fifteen long years in Italy in the Second Punic War, Hannibal never made a serious attempt to crack the core of Rome's alliance in central Italy.

To do so would have required a long, grinding exercise in siege warfare against Rome's key allies. Hannibal preferred maneuver warfare; he was a dancer, not a slugger. We can't say whether his decision not to engage in sieges evinces a failure more of technology, of culture, or of personal preference. In any case, he failed to change, and it cost him dearly.

In spite of Hannibal's presence in Italy for fifteen long years, in spite of defections by most of the peoples of southern and northern Italy, Rome's allies in central Italy remained loyal. That gave Rome the freedom to send expeditionary forces to Carthaginian Spain and eventually to conquer it. The leader of this effort was Publius Cornelius Scipio, later known as Scipio Africanus (236–183 BCE). Scipio was able to learn from Hannibal's tactics and apply them to the Roman military. Under Scipio's leadership, the Roman army changed from an old-fashioned infantry power to a state-of-the-art, combined-forces fighting machine.

Scipio's next move was diplomatic, and it was a coup—he won over the Numidian prince Masinissa to the side of Rome. Carthage fought back, and there was a domestic struggle involving different factions in Numidia, but, in the end, Rome got the country solidly on its side. Given the importance of Numidia's cavalry to Carthage's war-fighting abilities, this move was a game changer.

Scipio invaded North Africa in 204, thereby forcing Hannibal to leave Italy the next year and sail home. Scipio fought a set battle against Hannibal (the Battle of Zama, 202) where he outdid the master and destroyed Hannibal's army. Masinissa's Numidian cavalry tipped the balance and brought Scipio his victory. Carthage now surrendered and agreed to be a small state reined in to its North African homeland, weighted down once again by a huge indemnity.

Rome, meanwhile, had become a military giant. Before Hannibal's invasion it normally put six to eight legions (roughly thirty thousand men) in the field; during the Second Punic War it fielded up to twenty-eight legions (roughly 120,000 men) plus allied forces. It had added two million acres of public land to its control, confiscated from rebellious allies. It had acquired a new empire in Spain and a new ally in Numidia. By guiding the state to victory, the Roman Senate strengthened its ability to direct Roman policy. With Carthage reduced to second-rate status, no peer polity challenged Rome's domination of the central and western Mediterranean, although smaller states in Africa, Spain, and Gaul still posed a challenge. Rome was now ready to turn eastward. It took only a dozen years for it to defeat the two greatest powers of the Hellenistic Greek world, Macedon and Syria.

The Third Punic War began fifty-two years after the Second Punic War ended. The final conflict between Rome and Carthage was less a duel than a massacre. Carthage had recovered as a wealthy and vibrant city-state, but it was no threat. Rome feared an enemy revival nonetheless, so it decided to eliminate Carthage as a political entity. It gave the Carthaginians an ultimatum: either abandon their city and disperse or fight to the death.

The Carthaginians chose the latter, and the Romans sacked and destroyed the former queen of North Africa. The wars between Rome and Carthage came to their tragic end.

THE ROLE OF GEOGRAPHY IN THE CONFLICT

At first, geography helped keep Rome and Carthage from fighting. The two cities are about 325 nautical miles apart (calculating from Rome's port of Ostia), or about a four-day journey. Events brought the two sides closer. Once Rome conquered southern Italy and Carthage garrisoned Messana, the two powers faced each other across a body of water, the Strait of Messina, less than two miles wide at its narrowest point. The conquest of Sicily brought Rome closer to Carthage: the shortest sailing distance from the island to Carthage is about 130 nautical miles, or two days.[3]

Geography also engendered a false sense of security on both sides of the conflict. Most of the Punic Wars were fought far from Carthaginian territory. The First Punic War was waged mostly in Sicily, with an episode in North Africa, and the Second Punic War mostly in Spain, Italy, and Sicily until the final phase in North Africa. With most of the fighting taking place in other countries, it was all too easy for people in Carthage to consider the wars with Rome a foreign matter, largely to be left in the hands of the various generals who waged it.

When Carthage lost the First Punic War it gave up its navy, and the naval advantage passed to Rome. Hannibal's capital at New Carthage (modern Cartagena, Spain) was over a thousand miles away from Rome by land. It seemed hard to believe that Hannibal could invade Italy overland, given the obstacles of the Pyrenees Mountains, the Rhône River, and the Alps, and yet he did. He thereby forced Rome to give up the planned invasion of Carthage's home territory in Africa and to defend Italy instead.

More precisely, Rome postponed its invasion of North Africa for fourteen years, from 218 to 204. In the meantime, it maintained an offensive posture by continually sending armies and navies to Spain. It took twelve years, until 206, for Rome to succeed there, but it did at last drive Carthage from its overseas empire there. Meanwhile, geography did not prevent Hannibal's brother Hasdrubal from escaping Spain after suffering a major defeat there in 209 and marching overland to Italy, repeating his brother's earlier achievement. He faced an ambush in Italy, however, and was defeated and killed in battle (at the Metaurus, 207).

THE ROLE OF DYNAMIC LEADERS IN THE CONFLICT

The two sides produced their share of incompetent leaders. One thinks, for example, of Hanno, the Carthaginian commander of Messana who allowed himself to be captured by the Romans in 264 BCE and was forced to withdraw the Carthaginian garrison. His home government later had him crucified for poor judgment and cowardice. Or Gaius Terentius Varro and Lucius Aemilius Paullus, the two Roman commanders who led their army to a disastrous defeat at Cannae in 216 BCE. Paullus died in the battle; Varro lived to take almost sole blame, perhaps somewhat unfairly (Paullus had many friends).

Still, the conflicts also generated dynamic leaders. The First Punic War produced such Roman commanders as Gaius Duilius, victor of the naval battle at Mylae (260) and the first Roman to win a naval triumph, and Gaius Lutatius Catulus, who won the decisive victory at sea off the west coast of Sicily at the Aegates Islands that forced Carthage to sue for peace. It brought forth such generals on the Carthaginian side as Xanthippus, a Spartan mercenary commander who crushed a Roman army of invasion at the Battle of the Bagradas River near modern Tunis, in 255 BCE during the First Punic War, and Hamilcar Barca, the Carthaginian commander who raided Italy from his stronghold in northwestern Sicily and remained undefeated at the war's end.

The Second Punic War produced far more famous leaders. On the Roman side there was, for example, Fabius Maximus

"Cunctator" ("The Hesitator,") who in 217 held the office of "dic-tator," a six-month special magistrate endowed with full author-ity, whom Romans appointed only in times of emergency. Fabius stymied the enemy with a strategy of dogged harassment without risking a major battle, a ploy that worked for a short while until the Roman public demanded action. There was also Claudius Marcellus, a famously doughty warrior, winner of the *spolia opima* ("rich spoils") for defeating an enemy commander (a Gallic chief) in single combat in northern Italy several years before Hannibal's invasion. These spoils were the arms and armor stripped off the body of the slain enemy leader. During the Second Punic War, Marcellus conquered an important Carthaginian ally, the heav-ily fortified city of Syracusae (Syracuse) in Sicily, after a two-year siege (214–212).

Hamilcar Barca gave Carthage its three best generals in this war in the form of his sons: Hasdrubal, whose greatest success came in recapturing Spain from the Romans in 211; his younger brother, Mago, who commanded alongside Hasdrubal in 211 and who served successfully in the field during the invasion of Italy 218–216; and the greatest of the trio, Hannibal.

Hannibal is justly considered one of history's great captains. As Polybius wrote, Hannibal "was by his very nature truly a marvel-ous man, with a personality suited by its original constitution to carry out anything that lies within human affairs."[4] He shocked Rome by invading Italy after a nine-hundred-mile overland trek from southern Spain. He then proceeded to demonstrate his bril-liance and superiority as a field commander by defeating the Romans in a series of great battles, most notably at Cannae in Apu-lia in southern Italy. There on August 2, 216, Hannibal butchered a Roman army that was nearly twice the size of his. He inflicted on the Romans forty-eight thousand deaths and captured twenty thousand men. Hannibal saw six to eight thousand of his own soldiers killed, most of them from his allied troops—his least reli-able men. The Romans lost about 75 percent of their army while the Carthaginians lost only about 10 to 15 percent of theirs. It was one of the most stunning battlefield victories in history.

Unfortunately for himself and his country, Hannibal was not equally good at strategy. After failing to rouse his tired army after Cannae for a forced march and a coup de main on Rome, he lost what was probably his best opportunity to compel the enemy to make peace. Instead, he underestimated Rome's resilience, determination, and adaptability. An unsuccessful Hannibal still remained dangerous, and he kept his army in Italy for fifteen years. He was a sufficiently good leader that he never suffered a mutiny. That was not enough to win the war, however.

Rome soon produced a general who was able to learn from Hannibal's tactics and apply them to the Roman military: Scipio Africanus. Scipio came from an elite military and political family but he was not bound by tradition. He was shrewd, innovative, and a survivor—literally, as he lived on through the carnage of Cannae and rallied the other soldiers who had made it through; they elected him to be their commander. Scipio proceeded to rethink the way Rome fought wars, making the legions more flexible and embracing cunning and ruse.

Polybius labeled Scipio "perhaps the most illustrious man of any born before the present generation."[5] Scipio was self-assured and highly intelligent. He was a natural leader of men. Sober and religious, he used omens and the divine to encourage his men. Like Hannibal, he was a master of military surprise.

Both Scipio's father and uncle were killed in action against the enemy in Spain; because of not just his pedigree but his talent and promise, Scipio received the command as their successor, in spite of the Romans' preference for older and more experienced men in such positions. He did not disappoint: at the age of only twenty-six Scipio captured New Carthage, the Carthaginian capital of Spain. He then won two great set battles against Carthaginian armies (Baecula, 209, and Ilipa, 206) and drove Carthage from Spain. He next achieved a diplomatic coup by wooing away Hannibal's most important ally, Numidia. Ultimately Scipio invaded North Africa and forced Hannibal and his army to evacuate Italy and come home.

Hannibal is one of the most admired, most romantic, and most tragic military leaders in history. He took staggering risks that bore spectacular fruit only to have them turn sour in the end. Scipio is one of the most daring, cunning, and successful generals in history, but when it comes to the history books he stands in Hannibal's shadow.

Scipio plays Wellington to Hannibal's Napoleon. Or perhaps Scipio plays Grant to Hannibal's Lee, because there's a real analogy between the Punic Wars—especially the Second Punic War—and the American Civil War. In both conflicts one side pitted dash and dazzle on the battlefield against a duller but more disciplined state with greater staying power. In both cases, slow but steady won the race.

The Third Punic War should have been a one-sided struggle. A now much diminished Carthage tried to defend itself from destruction at the hands of a far superior Roman force. The Carthaginians did surprisingly well, handing the Romans several defeats, until the appointment of Scipio Aemilianus (ca. 184–129) to head the Roman expeditionary force. Scipio was a decorated military hero who had excelled in battle in Macedonia and in Spain. The war at Carthage took him a year of hard fighting but he finally succeeded in capturing the city, which he burned and razed. According to Polybius, Scipio Aemilianus was a sensitive man who felt a frisson of horror at the sight of Carthage in flames, imagining the same fate for Rome one day.[6] Perhaps that's true, or perhaps Polybius was just flattering his patron.

THE SIGNIFICANCE FOR SIMILAR CONTEMPORARY CONFLICTS

Rome and Carthage were both aggressive, militaristic republics bent on expanding their empires in the central and western Mediterranean. Carthage was more brilliant, but Rome had a stronger base. To the extent that we can reconstruct Carthaginian

politics—and admittedly, our ability to do so is limited—it appears
that Carthage was not as committed to victory as Rome was. But
we are on firmer ground in appreciating the superiority of Rome's
alliance system.

Allies were crucial. Wars are won not just on the battlefield but
also in embassies and foreign ministries or their ancient equiva-
lents. Stealing an enemy's vital ally, as Rome stole Numidia from
Carthage, can be the key to victory. The Germans did this in effect
in 1939 by weaning the Soviets from the British and French (only
then to throw away their success in a disastrous invasion of Russia less than two years later). America's successful entente with
China in the 1970s bought the United States only a fig leaf when it
came to ending the war in Vietnam—the United States still faced
defeat but a somewhat less humiliating defeat than it would have
had otherwise. Yet the US-China relationship paid dividends in
weakening the USSR and, ultimately, winning the Cold War for
the West.

Now that the US-China relationship faces rough waters, we can
extract a few lessons from Rome and Carthage's violent history.
To start with the obvious, war is terrible to contemplate. Antiquity had no weapons of mass destruction, but the rivalry literally
annihilated Carthage and did huge damage to the economy and
demography of Italy. It also set in train a series of events that, in
the long run, tested Rome's courage to make painful reforms in
order to save the republic—a test that Rome failed, with the result
being the monarchy of the Caesars. The wages of defeat in the
Punic Wars was death, but the price of victory was revolution.

War should only be considered as a very last resort. Much better to engage in rivalry by peaceful means, such as economics,
communications, and espionage. The wars between Carthage and
Rome offer a few principles for such rivalry. To begin with, understand the enemy and the ways in which it is different from your
own society. Correctly identify its weakest points and be sure that
you are able to target them. To put it another way, be prepared to
fight the conflict that is needed to win, not the conflict that you
feel comfortable engaging in. For all his achievements, Hannibal

notably failed to evaluate Rome and its alliance structure correctly; nor did he undertake the tactics (i.e., siegecraft) needed to defeat it.

Do not underestimate the enemy. Assume that, if the conflict lasts long enough, it will eventually learn to copy anything you can do. Learn how to fight the way the other side does. Rome learned to master Hannibal's new way of warfare, deploying on the battlefield a sophisticated combined-arms military. Bring the struggle to the enemy's ground but only if you have defended your own home turf sufficiently. Rome paid heavily during the Second Punic War for its failure to take Hannibal seriously enough.

Ensure that you have a unified and coordinated team. The political leadership, the legislators, the finance ministry, the military, and the intelligence services all have to work together. Both sides suffered from times of disunity. Other Roman leaders, for example, reversed Fabius's strategy of avoiding a conventional battle with Hannibal, and the disastrous result was Cannae. Carthage's home government, to take another case, did not send Hannibal the reinforcements he requested in Italy, to Carthage's cost.

Look to your allies, and make sure that the ties binding the most important of them to you are strong and firm enough to survive a conflict. Always have an eye on the enemy's chief allies and consider what it would take to wean them away. For all of Carthage's sophistication, it was Rome that proved shrewder in alliance management.

Finally, study history. That should be obvious, but in an era when old seems boring and when academic historians have largely lost interest in politics and war, it bears stating.

RECOMMENDATIONS FOR FURTHER READING

For the ancient literary sources in translation, see Polybius, Ian Scott-Kilvert, and F. W. Walbank, *The Rise of the Roman Empire* (Harmondsworth, UK: Penguin, 2003), and Livy, Aubrey De

Sélincourt, and Betty Radice, *The War with Hannibal: Books XXI–XXX of the History of Rome from Its Foundation* (Harmondsworth, UK: Penguin, 2004). Translations of the other ancient sources can be found in the Loeb Classical Library Series and are online.[7] For an introduction to the Roman Republic, see Michael H. Crawford, *The Roman Republic* (Cambridge, MA: Harvard University Press, 1982); for an introduction to Carthage, see Richard Miles, *Carthage Must Be Destroyed: The Rise and Fall of an Ancient Civilization* (New York: Viking, 2011). An excellent reference work is B. D. Hoyos, ed., *A Companion to the Punic Wars* (Malden, MA: Wiley-Blackwell, 2011). For an introduction to the wars between Rome and Carthage, see Hoyos, *Mastering the West: Rome and Carthage at War* (New York: Oxford University Press, 2015), as well as Nigel Bagnall, *The Punic Wars: Rome, Carthage and the Struggle for the Mediterranean* (London: Pimlico, 1999), and Adrian Goldsworthy, *The Punic Wars* (London: Cassell, 2000).

For military histories of the Punic Wars, see J. F. Lazenby, *The First Punic War: A Military History* (Stanford, CA: Stanford University Press, 1996), and Lazenby, *Hannibal's War: A Military History of the Second Punic War* (Warminster, UK: Aris & Phillips, 1978). On Cannae, the most famous battle of the Punic Wars, see Adrian Goldsworthy, *Cannae* (London: Cassell Military, 2001), and Robert L. O'Connell, *The Ghosts of Cannae: Hannibal and the Darkest Hour of the Roman Republic* (New York: Random House, 2010).

Two recent and fine biographies of Hannibal are Patrick Hunt, *Hannibal* (New York: Simon & Schuster, 2017), and John Prevas, *Hannibal's Oath: The Life and Wars of Rome's Greatest Enemy* (Boston: Da Capo Press, 2017). On Scipio Africanus, see B. H. Liddell Hart, *Scipio Africanus: Greater than Napoleon* (Boston: Da Capo Press, 2004). I compare Hannibal to Alexander and Caesar in Barry Strauss, *Masters of Command: Alexander, Hannibal, Caesar, and the Genius of Leadership* (New York: Simon & Schuster, 2012).

NOTES

1. For a preliminary assessment of some important underwater archaeological finds from the First Punic War, see Sebastiano Tusa and Jeffrey Royal,

"The Landscape of the Naval Battle at the Egadi Islands (241 B.C.)," *Journal of Roman Archaeology* 25 (2012): 7–48. For a discussion of Hannibal's route over the Alps, see Patrick Hunt, *Hannibal* (New York: Simon & Schuster, 2017), 53–73.

2. Polybius, *Histories* 1.59, in trans. Evelyn S. Shuckburgh (London, New York: Macmillan, 1889; reprint Bloomington, IN, 1962).

3. For the distances, see http://stanford.orbis.edu.

4. Polybius, *Histories* 9.22.6.

5. Polybius, *Histories* 10.2.2.

6. Polybius, *Histories* 38.21–22.

7. For example, at http://www.perseus.tufts.edu or http://penelope.uchicago.edu/Thayer/E/Roman/Texts/home.html.

3

A STRATEGIC CAMPAIGN: THE BYZANTINE EMPEROR HERAKLEIOS DESTROYS SASANIAN PERSIA

Edward N. Luttwak

The largest and boldest strategic offensive in the entire history of the Byzantine or Eastern Roman Empire was undertaken, in the year 627 and under the most desperate circumstances, to rescue the empire from imminent destruction. It ended a year later, with the total defeat of Sasanian Persia.

The Roman and Sasanian Empires had been fighting each other for some four centuries—necessarily inconclusively, because the Romans never even tried to conquer their way across the entire Iranian plateau, and the Sasanians had never even tried to conquer Constantinople to finish off the empire.

The two empires would instead fight over the control of the Armenian, Caucasian, and Mesopotamian borderlands between them, and especially the great fortified border cities: Edessa (Riha to local Kurds, Şanlıurfa on Turkish maps), Nisibis, Dara, and Amida (preserved in the Kurdish Amed, but Diyarbakır in Turkish), which changed hands several times—the particularly dramatic siege of 359 is described in uniquely expert detail by the fine historian and military officer Ammianus Marcellinus.

Between their wars, Byzantines and Sasanians recognized each other as civilized antagonists, negotiated detailed peace treaties once the fighting stopped, and coexisted peacefully (until the next

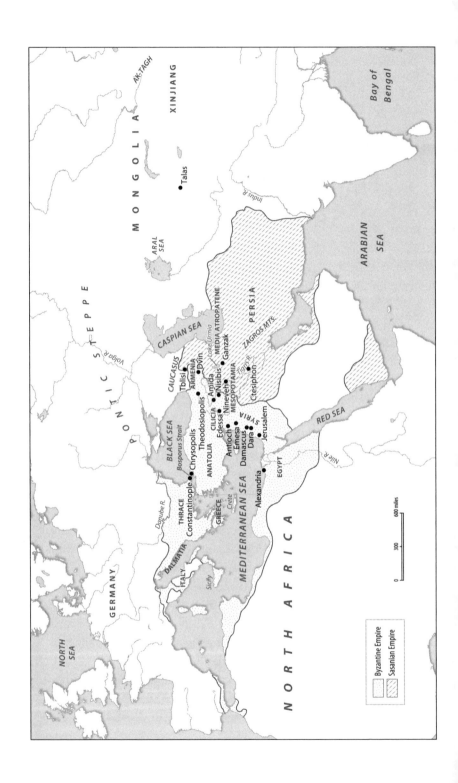

NORTH SEA

GERMANY

DALMATIA

ITALY

Sicily

Danube R.

THRACE

Constantinople

GREECE

Crete

Bosporus Strait

BLACK SEA

Chrysopolis

ANATOLIA

Theodosiopolis

CILICIA

Antioch

Edessa

Emesa

Damascus

Dara

SYRIA

Jerusalem

MEDITERRANEAN SEA

Alexandria

EGYPT

NORTH AFRICA

Nile R.

RED SEA

PONTIC STEPPE

Volga R.

CAUCASUS

Tblisi

ARMENIA

Dvin

Amida

Nisibis

Nineveh

MESOPOTAMIA

Lake Urmia

Ganzak

MEDIA ATROPATENE

Tigris R.

Ctesiphon

ZAGROS MTS.

PERSIA

CASPIAN SEA

ARAL SEA

MONGOLIA

XINJIANG

Ak-Tagh

Talas

Indus R.

Bay of Bengal

ARABIAN SEA

0   300   600 miles

Byzantine Empire

Sasanian Empire

war). Their rulers could also trust each other in delicate matters.
That, paradoxically, provided the ostensible excuse for the longest
and last war that was started in the year 603 by the Sasanian ruler
Khosrow II, who launched the most ambitious of all Sasanian
invasions, very much in the role of the "ascendant power" that
seeks to abrogate the prior balance of power.

Khosrow wanted to conquer much more than borderlands
and border cities—he wanted everything, ostensibly because of
the illegitimacy of the Byzantine emperor of the day, the usurper
Phokas, who had recently seized power by mutiny. A mere
hekatontarchos—a commander of a hundred, a captain at best in
modern terms, if not just a company sergeant major—Phokas had
murdered his predecessor Maurikios (582–602), whom Khosrow
could rightfully claim as his patron and political father: as a young
man, he had been sheltered at Maurikios's imperial court from the
deadly intrigues of Sasanian palace politics.

Khosrow set out to conquer the empire as a whole, supposedly
also to propagate the dualist Zoroastrian cult of Ahura Mazda,
"God of Light and Goodness," which had once competed with
Christianity within the Roman Empire with considerable success.
After four centuries of intermittent limited wars, it was total war.

In Constantinople, the unpopular Phokas was unable to mount
an effective defense. After an initial phase, in which Sasanian
armies conquered the Mesopotamian border region including
wealthy Edessa in 610–611, Sasanian armies entered Syria and
conquered Antioch (modern-day Antakya), one of the largest cities of the empire. In 613 they seized Emesa (now Homs, Syria)
and Damascus, then descending to capture Jerusalem in May 614.
Never before had Persian conquests reached that far, but what
happened next was much worse: the invasion of Egypt, the largest
single source of Byzantine tax revenues and grain supplies. In 619
even the capital Alexandria had fallen, completing the conquest.

Another Sasanian army threatened the survival of the empire
even more directly by penetrating into its core territory of Anatolia. By 611 it won a major victory at Caesarea of Cappadocia
(Kayseri), and in 626 a Sasanian force reached all the way west

to Chrysopolis (now Üsküdar), directly opposite Constantinople on the Asiatic shore across the Bosporus, at that point less than a mile wide.

Nor could the Byzantines concentrate their forces against the Persians because another formidable enemy had arrived from the Eurasian steppes to cross the Danube, invade Thrace, and invest Constantinople: the Avars.

The first steppe power of great consequence since Attila's Huns, they were formed in the usual way of ethnogenesis around an Inner Asian core, probably the Juan-juan of the Chinese sources, which acquired Turkic and other camp followers as they won victories and moved westward.

By 557 the Avars had crossed the Volga and had started moving west across the Pontic steppe north of the Black Sea. Three years later, they sent an envoy to Constantinople whose name is recorded as Kandikh. Unintimidated by the vastness of the city—unimaginably grand for a nomadic tent-dweller—or the magnificence of the court, Kandikh declared that the Avars were all-powerful and could easily destroy all who stood in their path, before suggesting "an alliance" with the Roman state in exchange for valuable gifts, yearly payments, and very fertile land to inhabit.

The boasting had a basis. Like the Huns before them, the Avars had mounted archers with powerful composite bows, but they also had much more: heavy cavalry to charge with the lance (to drive enemies into dense formations, into which the mounted archers could launch volleys of arrows); a superior form of body armor, possibly of Chinese origin; the stirrup, a major innovation in itself; and most important, a cadre of skilled engineers to construct siege engines including mobile fighting towers and powerful trebuchets. Constantinople's Theodosian Wall system, with its moat, three separate walls, and strongly built fighting towers, had been an impassable barrier for all their steppe predecessors, but could offer no such assurance against the much more accomplished Avars who arrived in July 626.

Moreover, like other successful steppe campaigners before and after them, the Avars had gathered a much larger mass of other warriors around their own elite forces, in this case Germanic Gepids and Slavs in great numbers.

Finally, the Avars must also have had intelligence and diplomatic skills, because they invested Constantinople from the European side just when the Sasanian army that had advanced across Anatolia reached the Asiatic shore in front of the city.

With enthusiastic popular participation Phokas had been overthrown in 610 by the son of the highest official in Latin-speaking North Africa, Flavius Heraclius, Herakleios to the Greeks. The new emperor commanded only besieged Constantinople, Greece and its islands, uninvaded tracts of Anatolia, and some thinly garrisoned coastal tracts of North Africa, Sicily, Italy, and Dalmatia—none of them rich sources of revenues or recruits, especially in the wake of the catastrophic visitations of *Yersinia pestis* since 541. Justinian's plague had interrupted the marvelous resurgence of imperial power, killing off as much as half the population, with losses among soldiers and officials even higher, disrupting the machinery of empire.

The imperial treasury, the true engine of all power, was exhausted. *The Chronicle of Theophanes* records extreme measures in the year 620/1: "Being short of funds he [Herakleios] took on loan the moneys of religious establishments and he also took the candelabra and other vessels of the holy ministry from the Great Church, which he minted into a great quantity of gold and silver coin."[1]

Threatened from two sides, with much-diminished revenues and afflicted by recurrent plague, Constantinople was a most precarious base for the extraordinary strategic campaign that resulted in total victory in 628. Moreover, the new emperor inherited an army much attenuated, with few troops, and mostly in a miserable state because Byzantine forces had been battered again and again, in almost two decades of defeats, retreats, and outright collapses of frontier and city defenses.

It was mostly fragments of units, individual veterans, and new recruits who rallied to Herakleios and his purse, so after assembling them, and arousing their religious resentment ("You see, O my brethren and children, how the enemies of God have trampled

upon our land, have laid our cities waste, have burnt our sanctu-
aries . . . how they defile . . . our churches"[2]), the emperor set out
to train his troops.

Systematic step-by-step training with a fixed program of
instruction was one ancient Roman tradition that had survived.
Herakleios led his men through individual combat skill training and then unit drills followed by full-scale battle exercises in
complete formations. Theophanes records that "[Herakleios] . . .
formed two armed contingents. . . . When he had securely mar-
shalled the two companies he bade them attack each other: there
were violent collisions and mutual conflict, and a semblance of
war was to be seen. One could observe a frightening sight, yet one
without the fear of danger, murderous clashes without blood."[3]

Next came diplomacy. With Persians on one side and Avars on
the other, Herakleios tried to detach the latter from the alliance
but was almost captured himself when he tried to negotiate with
the Avar paramount ruler, the khagan.

His attempt to appease Khosrow II had failed long before. The
Chronicon Paschale records under the year 615 that after the loss of
Syria and the fall of Jerusalem, when the first Persian incursion
through Anatolia had reached the shore opposite Constantinople,
Herakleios sent a letter to Khosrow, accepting his overlordship,
whereby Byzantium would become a client-state under the Sasanian system of indirect rule:

> [With] confidence in . . . God and in your majesty, [we] have sent
> [to you] your slaves Olympius the most glorious former consul,
> patrician and praetorian prefect, and Leontius the most glorious
> former consul, patrician and city prefect, and Anastasius the most
> God-loved presbyter [of Hagia Sophia] and *syncellus*; we beseech
> that they may be received in appropriate manner by your super-
> abundant Might, and that they shortly return to us, securing for us
> the peace which is pleasing to God and appropriate to your peace-
> loving Might. We beg too of your clemency to consider Heraclius,
> our most pious emperor, as a true son, one who is eager to perform
> the service of your Serenity in all things.[4]

Appeasement failed, yet no attack on Constantinople ensued because Khosrow's armies were instead diverted to Egypt, of much greater economic value than besieged Constantinople, and also much easier to conquer. Khosrow's reply is only recorded in the Armenian history of Sebeos, and may be a fabrication because its wording seems calculated to stiffen Byzantine resistance:

> Khosrov, honoured among the gods, lord and king of all the earth, and offspring of the great Aramazd [Ahura Mazda], to Heraclius our senseless and insignificant servant. . . . Having collected an army of brigands, you give me no rest. So did I not destroy the Greeks? But you claim to trust in your God. Why did he not save Caesarea [of Cappadocia] and Jerusalem and the great Alexandria [of Egypt] from my hands? Do you not know that I have subjected to myself the sea and the dry land? So it is only Constantinople that I shall not be able to erase?[5]

The suspicion of forgery is enhanced by an offer of generous terms for Herakleios himself, thereby suggesting that his persistence in war was selfless: "However, I shall forgive you all your trespasses. 'Arise, take your wife and children and come here. I shall give you estates, vineyards and olive-trees whereby you may make a living.'. . . Let not your vain hope deceive you."

Failed diplomacy was thus converted into useful propaganda.

With that, all was set for Herakleios to launch a counteroffensive against Sasanian Persia, on March 25, 624. At the time, Constantinople was not yet besieged as it would be in 626, and Sasanian strength was divided by multiple advances into Anatolia, with many troops still in Egypt and Syria.

The safe course would have been to push back the Sasanian armies step by step across the length of Anatolia and back into Mesopotamia—except that all the candelabra and vessels of all the churches of Constantinople could not have paid for an army large enough to advance by sheer strength in a frontal offensive. Moreover, even if successful initially—unlikely given the ratio of forces—a frontal offensive could not have long succeeded, because Sasanian forces scattered in Egypt and Syria would have been called to oppose it.

Herakleios instead led his army in a deep-penetration offensive or, if one prefers, a strategic raid all the way east through Anatolia into what was then Armenia and is now northeast Turkey, to eventually reach the original Sasanian heartland in what is now northwest Iran.

That was a high-risk maneuver in itself, but it also required accepting the greater risk of leaving Constantinople with only its wall garrison and the depleted imperial fleet to defend it against the Avars arriving on its European side, and the Sasanian forces gathering on the Anatolian shore.

The army of Herakleios seems to have been little resisted as it sidestepped the Sasanian force directly across the Bosporus to land in Anatolia and march through it to Theodosiopolis (Erzurum) and then beyond it into Armenia, capturing and looting Dvin, now in northeast Turkey, before reaching and destroying the great Zoroastrian temple at Takht-i-Suleiman, extinguishing the eternal fire of Vshnasp, as Sebeos called it (more correctly Adur Gushnasp), near the modern Ganzak, the Greek Gazaca, capital of Media Atropatene, in modern western Azerbaijan, still within Iran at this time (despite a separatist movement).

It was perhaps revenge for the burning of the Jerusalem churches in 614, but much more likely it was a calculated move designed to provoke Khosrow into a frantic and ill-prepared response, because Adur Gushnasp was the sanctuary of his dynasty, which claimed priestly authority—it was named after Sasan, great priest of the Temple of Anahita and grandfather of Ardashir, the founder of the Sasanian Empire, whose rulers were consecrated before that same "royal" fire of Adur Gushnasp.

Of course, Khosrow had to react to the counterinvasion, but he obviously did not take the threat very seriously because he sent separate and uncoordinated Sasanian forces to try to intercept the fast-moving Herakleios. The latter's men defeated at least one Sasanian force, led by the most distinguished of Sasanian field commanders, Shahrbaraz, before encamping for the winter.

Herakleios did not attempt to persist in his deep-penetration offensive, no doubt because his army, though obviously well trained, battle hardened, and victorious until then, was just too small. Thus in March 625 the Byzantine expeditionary force retreated from the Armenian highlands to the plains of southeast Anatolia, crossing through the Cilician Gates (modern Turkey's Gülek Bogazi).

Sasanian forces in pursuit from different directions were strung out and could not combine forces against the more mobile forces of Herakleios—who thus successfully implemented the operational method recommended for outnumbered forces in the military manual *Peri Strategikes*.

This war of movement was conducted within Anatolia, whose mountain terrain is interrupted by fertile, well-watered valleys, with the coastal plains of Cappadocia and Cilicia even more productive. That allowed Herakleios to feed his army with locally collected taxes and contributions from churches and monasteries, indispensable because besieged Constantinople itself precariously supplied by sea could send him nothing.

Fighting came to an end as winter approached. Herakleios could not have stopped when the cold weather arrived if Khosrow's troops had not already stopped before him. It was not that they were less hardy, but their horses needed fodder to survive after October, so they had to retreat to winter quarters where they stored fodder, staying there until the spring growth of new grass.

This was a logistical detail that became absolutely crucial in the ensuing events. In the winter of 626, the army of Herakleios did not seek shelter in well-stocked quarters as it had done in 624 and then again in 625. Instead Herakleios led his forces eastward into the Caucasus, on his way to the Persian heartland. Byzantine horses were no different from those of the Sasanians, but very different horses did exist, and would soon arrive on the scene.

When Herakleios abandoned his capital city to campaign offensively, the Avars and their camp followers already threatened the city, as did the Sasanian forces gathering across the narrow Bosporus. That was extremely risky, of course, but it was not until June 29, 626, that the danger reached its maximum intensity when the city came under the convergent attack of the Avars with their siege engines, their Slav camp followers in boats, and the Sasanian army of Shahrbaraz. According to the *Chronicon Paschale*:

> [Some Avars] approached the venerated church of the Holy Maccabees [in Galata, across the narrow Golden Horn from Constantinople]; they made themselves visible to the Persians, who had congregated in the region of Chrysopolis, and they made their presence known to each other by fire signals.[6]

Both Avars and Persians had been there before, but separately. In June 626 it was different—they concerted their moves, according to the chronicler Theophanes: "As for Sarbaros [Shahrbaraz, the Sasanian commander], he [Khosrow] dispatched him with his remaining army against Constantinople with a view to establishing an alliance between the Western Huns [Avars] and the . . . Slavs, and so advancing on the City and laying siege to it."[7]

That still required the operational coordination of the two armies—and armies in any case could not invest maritime Constantinople very effectively, as it projected into the sea with only a narrow landward side, which was very strongly fortified. Neither the Sasanians nor the Avars had warships, but the khagan had a substitute: he sent his Slav camp followers to attack the seaward side of the city that faces the Golden Horn in their *monoxyla*, one-tree dugouts. The same small boats were to ferry Sasanian troops across from the Asian shore. On that side, the city was fortified with nothing more than a seawall, very much weaker than the Theodosian Wall system. The Slavs were much more numerous than the Avars, and their boats "filled the gulf of the Horn with an immense multitude, beyond all number, whom they had brought from the Danube."

But the *monoxyla* were no match for the galleys and skiffs of the Byzantine navy with their skilled crews and embarked bowmen. The successive defeats that had deprived the empire of its most valuable provinces and much of its army had evidently inflicted much less damage to its navy, sustained as it was by the seafarers of coastal North Africa, southern Spain, Sicily, Italy, Crete, Cyprus, and the Aegean islands. Though hugely outnumbered, the navy fought off wave after wave of small boats, killing their crews, until August 7, 626, the day when both Avars and Sasanians gave up their sieges.

Having failed to seize the city and having certainly eaten out the surroundings during the siege, the Avars and surviving Slavs had to raid elsewhere for their food, while the Sasanian troops retreated in pursuit of Herakleios, whose war of movement that had started in March 624 changed drastically in the autumn of 627.

Once again he advanced eastward into the Caucasus, and was no doubt expected to retreat once again with the approach of winter. But this time his endeavor was not a large-scale raid, but rather a full-scale, deep-penetration offensive. That required a larger force than Herakleios could command, and also horses that could somehow find pasture in the winter. He received both, as much earlier events came to fruition at that critical time.

Two generations earlier, in 567, Maniakh, himself a Sogdian—an inhabitant of the nation of city dwellers and caravan leaders who ranged across Central Asia and beyond—had appeared at the Byzantine court to introduce an envoy sent by the Turkic ruler of a vast steppe empire until then unknown in Byzantium. The bureau of translators facilitated the talks—they had Sogdian interpreters. The envoy brought a gift of Chinese silk and offered its direct sale, bypassing Sasanian Persia, but commerce was not the priority, because he listed the tribes subject to his empire, asked for peace, and offered an offensive and defensive alliance implicitly aimed at the Sasanians.

The emperor Justin II (565–578) evidently saw the strategic opportunity. He sent his envoy Zemarchos on a three-year mission to Sir Yabghu Khagan Ishtemi, ruler of the western part of the vast Turkic Khaganate (which is now the subject of nationalist ravings in Turkey, with even less justification than Mussolini's claim to Roman martial virtues).

Born of a 552 revolt against their Juan-juan masters in Mongolia (probably the Avars), the khaganate empire had expanded at a phenomenal rate, engulfing dozens of nomadic tribes as well as the settled populations of river valleys and oasis cities across Inner Asia.

As with both earlier and later mounted archers of the Eurasian steppe, tactical strength could be elevated into strategic power by charismatic and skillful chiefs who could unify clans, tribes, and nations to fight together instead of fighting each other. The Yabghu Khagan Ishtemi was the son of one such, the T'u-wu of the Chinese sources, who had united many Turkic tribes, and brother of his successor, the senior ruler Bumin in direct charge of the eastern portion of the empire.

Of all the steppe powers that emerged from central and northeast Asia, this first Turkic state was the largest but for the Mongol six centuries later, and its westward expansion inevitably collided with the northern outposts of the Sasanian Persian Empire. Its containment was always the highest Byzantine strategic priority, and in August 569 Zemarchos was sent to "Sizabul," as the source calls the khagan, to take up his offer of an alliance.

After a dangerous journey that started by sailing to the far side of the Black Sea to cross two thousand miles of what is now southern Russia, southern Kazakhstan, and Uzbekistan, it was another thousand miles or so in a straight line to the seat of Sizabul, in a valley of the Ak-tagh (translated as "golden mountain" in the Greek text, but probably "white mountain") in the Altai region where modern China, Kazakhstan, and Mongolia converge, though there is another equally distant "white mountain" on the outer edge of modern China's Xinjiang region. A minor detail in the surviving account by Menander is our certain evidence that Zemarchos had reached that far east: it describes a shamanistic ceremony otherwise unknown to Byzantine culture but typical of northeast Asia.[8]

Zemarchos's mission was successful: Sizabul even invited him to join him in an expedition to Talas (now Taraz in the Zhambyl region of southern Kazakhstan) to parley with the Persians for the sole purpose of effecting a break in relations. After another strenuous return journey home, it is reported, Zemarchos communicated with the emperor and "told him everything."

That was the source of the powerful reinforcements that Herakleios received when his autumn expedition reached the Caucasus in 627. Riding their small, hardy Mongol horses that could find pasture even under the snow, "40,000 brave men" joined the Byzantine army. It was "Ziebel" who sent them, according to Theophanes, but that was either the Tong Yabghu who ruled the western khaganate of the Turkic empire, or the head of the Khazar khaganate that was emerging from its disintegration. Either way they were enemies of Sasanian Persia, and hereditary enemies of the Avars who had just failed to take Constantinople and whom they denigrated as fit only to be "trampled under the hooves of our horses, like ants."

Evidently Herakleios was a very great field commander who had survived against the odds in three years of mobile campaigning, but with thousands of formidable mounted archers added to his forces he could finally become a victorious commander. Setting out from Tbilisi in September 627, Herakleios advanced in a vast turning movement hinged on Lake Urmia, now in northwest Iran, to then move south, crossing the Great Zab River to reach Nineveh (now Mosul, Iraq) by the Tigris River.

For three years Khosrow had sent armies to pursue the outnumbered Herakleios, but on December 12, 627, it was a greatly reinforced Herakleios who chose to give battle. The Armenian history of Sebeos offers a glimpse of the fighting, just enough to recognize the tactical style of Herakleios—first maneuver to confuse the enemy to achieve surprise, then attack: "Joining forces [the Sasanians] pursued Heraclius. But Heraclius drew them on as far as the plain of Nineveh; then he turned back to attack them with great force. There was mist on the plain, and the Persian army did not realize that Heraclius had turned against them until they encountered each other . . . [the Byzantines] massacred them to a man."[9]

It was important to deplete Sasanian strength, but more decisive was the successful penetration into the deep rear of the hugely expanded territory conquered by Khosrow. Herakleios could strike at the vital centers of Sasanian power in what is now central

Iraq while the armies of Khosrow were still scattered across the wide arc of his conquests from remote Egypt to Syria and into Anatolia. The Sasanian capital was in Ctesiphon some thirty kilometers south of modern Baghdad, on the Tigris River some four hundred kilometers south of Nineveh, which Herakleios had just conquered.

Had the Sasanians not been certain that Herakleios would again retreat in winter as he had done each year until then, they could certainly have withdrawn enough troops from Egypt, Syria, and Anatolia in October and November to defend their core territory. But now it was too late.

In Nineveh, moreover, the Byzantine army and its Turkic allies captured Khosrow's palatial complex of gardens stocked with food and livestock, including exotic animals, all meat on the hoof for hungry troops ("in one enclosure there were 300 corn-fed ostriches, and in another about 500 corn-fed gazelles, and in another 100 corn-fed wild asses [onagers], . . . they also found sheep, pigs and oxen without number, and the whole army rested contentedly"). It was the Persian *paradeis,* "our paradise," in this case a vast walled garden filled with plants and animals that did duty for a palace under the Sasanians as with the Persian rulers before them.

Moving south toward Ctesiphon, the victorious army overran another palace complex at Dastagird with more exotic booty for the pot; palace officials were captured here, which indicates a rapid advance. Evidently there was no nearby replacement for the Sasanian army defeated at Nineveh.

In itself, the advance of the Byzantine army down the Tigris valley toward Ctesiphon need not have been catastrophic for Khosrow. He still had large forces at his command in the vast territories he had conquered, and his field commander Shahrbaraz was not very far away, in Syria, with a large army that could have returned to defend the empire's capital.

But it seems that constant warfare for over a quarter of a century had finally exhausted the Sasanian ruling elite and some of Khosrow's own family. To wage war with Byzantium was established practice for the dynasty. To wage total war to conquer the entire empire was utterly unprecedented. Herakleios supposedly stimulated these sentiments by making a peace offer that Khosrow supposedly rejected: "For it is not of my free will that I am burning Persia, but constrained by you. Let us, therefore, throw down our arms even now and embrace peace. Let us extinguish the fire before it consumes everything." The chronicler adds, "But [Khosrow] did not accept these proposals, and so the hatred of the Persian people grew against him."[10]

In a final move, Khosrow, by now certainly back in his Ctesiphon palace, sent out his "retainers, noblemen and servants" to fight the battle-hardened veterans at the gates. On February 23, 628, when Herakleios seemed to be on the verge of entering the city and finishing off the empire, Khosrow was overthrown and killed in a coup d'état by his own son Kawadh-Siroy, who opened talks and offered a prisoner exchange.

What ensued was not a capitulation but a negotiation—there were still large Sasanian armies in the field whose return could have tipped the balance. Instead of entering Ctesiphon—at some thirty square kilometers, its sheer size was probably intimidating to his small army—Herakleios moved more than three hundred miles northeast, returning to the familiar terrain of Takht-i-Suleiman (now Ganzak) in the foothills of the Zagros Mountains in April 628.

Kawadh-Siroy was himself overthrown in a military coup d'état by Shahrbaraz with whom Herakleios had exchanged messages for years in the attempt to detach him from his master. That facilitated negotiations that soon restored all the lost provinces to Byzantine rule but for the borderland along the Euphrates, which had long been Sasanian.

Having come to power when the empire was in immediate danger of extinction by the converging Avar and Sasanian forces, Herakleios did not have the military strength to drive back either one, let alone both. He did have enough strength to resist them within the walls of the city, and on the waters just in front of it—but not to restore an empire very largely submerged by enemy invaders. The combined attack of July 626 could have ended the span of Byzantium, 578 years before its catastrophic sack in 1204 at Christian hands, which eventually led to its final defeat in 1453. Even after the naval victory that saved the city from immediate conquest in 626, reserves of food and coin were dwindling, as was the imperial authority that alone preserved Byzantine rule in its unconquered but largely ungarrisoned territories.

Overcoming the temptation of (dutifully) remaining at his post within the sturdy walls of his capital, Herakleios instead embarked on a high-risk, *relational* maneuver on a theater-wide scale—a historical rarity in military history, with no comparable precedents or subsequent examples.

The risk part was built in: the campaign was another anabasis, a long-distance expedition without a sustaining base, and without a safe zone into which to retreat in the face of greatly superior forces. In this case, moreover, the anabasis was not headed to a longed-for and safe refuge, but away from it, leaving behind the imperial homeland even as it was besieged.

As for the "relational" quality of the campaign, that refers to a specific kind of military action that avoids frontal battles of attrition strength on strength, to instead sidestep or circumvent enemy strengths while seeking to exploit enemy weaknesses. Only in that way can materially inferior forces ever prevail, albeit at the cost of unavoidable operational risks—because strong enemy forces need not remain passive when circumvented and can themselves strike hard at exposed flanks, and weak enemy forces about to be attacked can suddenly be reinforced to turn the tables on the attacker.

In this case, the specific enemy weakness that Herakleios set out to exploit was the unexamined and unwarranted certitude on the Sasanian side that there was no strategic danger to be faced, that the Byzantine army could only mount irritating raids, which did not call for anything so drastic as the abandonment of new conquests to return home to defend the imperial core. This was therefore not an inherent Sasanian weakness but one induced by three years of inconclusive seasonal raids by small Byzantine forces that only lasted until winter, leaving the strategic situation unchanged with Constantinople still besieged and Ctesiphon still quite safe. The Byzantine raids could be painful, as in the case of the destruction of the Zoroastrian temple at Takht-i-Suleiman, a blow to the prestige of Khosrow and his dynasty. But Khosrow evidently decided that even very damaging raids did not justify the cost of the only reliable remedy, which was to withdraw Sasanian forces from the newly conquered lands of Syria and Egypt and instead use them to guard the old borders of the empire and its core territory in Mesopotamia. It would have meant nullifying Khosrow's great achievement—his unprecedented conquests of Byzantine territories.

Still, had the Sasanians known that the long-dormant Turkic alliance would suddenly be activated in a most powerful form, to multiply their enemy's strength with great numbers of steppe horsemen, they would have withdrawn from the west. But everything happened at light-cavalry speed, much too fast to react in time.

Thus, in the crucial year 627, the Sasanians did not withdraw from the west because they were sure that Herakleios would himself withdraw. He did not, and the result was the end of the last authentically Persian dynasty. Utterly enfeebled, Sasanian Iran would soon fall to Muslim raiders, thereby launching a miraculous god-given victory myth that was to last powerfully for centuries, and which lingers still as a very costly delusion, after countless defeats, of which the very first was inflicted by the Byzantines in 678, when they destroyed the fleet and repelled the army of Caliph Mu'awiya, armed with the confidence lastingly enhanced by the spectacular victory of Herakleios, and the new invention of Greek fire.

RECOMMENDATIONS FOR FURTHER READING

In the so-called plague of Justinian that started in 541, the bacterium *Yersinia pestis* probably killed half the population of the

Roman Empire, wrecking its institutions and greatly impoverishing its culture. Instead of the full-scale histories, ample documentation, and eloquent buildings that illuminate the sixth century—we can reconstruct not only events but personalities—the seventh left us nothing more than chronicles written by churchmen of one sort or another. The most continuous (284–813), if sparse, account is rendered into English as *The Chronicle of Theophanes Confessor*, now available in a splendid edition with a valuable commentary by Cyril Mango and Roger Scott (Oxford: Clarendon Press, 1997). The relevant part begins with the year 6102 since the creation, 609/10 in our years (p. 427), and the momentous arrival of the providential Turkic horsemen, somewhat misidentified as the Chazars, is recorded under the year 6117, our 624/5, on page 446.

Even more sparse, but with indispensable sections, is the *Chronicon Paschale* which ends in 628, just after the climax of the epic war; it too is available in English in a Liverpool University Press edition (1989), in its immensely useful "Translated Texts for Historians" series (vol. 7), translated with some notes by the Byzantinists Michael Whitby and Mary Whitby (the relevant part starts under Olympiad 348—even churchmen were classicizing in those years—our year 612, when Jerusalem fell to the Sasanians).

Not entirely duplicative of these two is the very brief *Nikephoros, Patriarch of Constantinople: Short History*, translated with a commentary by Cyril Mango and published by Dumbarton Oaks (1990) with the edited Greek text facing the English translation (all of us interested in Byzantium revere the Dumbarton Oaks god that offers the best library in the universe for their subject, with additional devotions paid for each one of its editions of texts never so well edited before, if available at all in printed form). The relevant part is at the very start (p. 35).

Rather more exotic is the Syriac-language chronicle now published as *Dionysius Reconstituted*, in which events are recorded under Seleucid years (some three hundred years ahead), starting at page 121 of *The Seventh Century in the West-Syrian Chronicles*, another Liverpool University Press achievement ("Translated

Texts for Historians," vol. 15, 1993) translated and annotated by Andrew Palmer.

Just as the Syriac source is necessary for the end of the story, for it includes the emergence of Muhammad and his followers, the Armenian historian whose writings are now available under the title *The Armenian History Attributed to Sebeos* (Liverpool: Liverpool University Press, "Translated Texts for Historians," vol. 31, 1999), translated and annotated by R. W. Thomson, provides the unique perspective of those caught in the middle. He does display a definite preference for the Byzantine side, not merely because of religious solidarity but because Herakleios really was the reasonable one—under his first regnal year, the Sebeos text records his immediate attempt to give peace a chance: "When Heraclius became king he sent messengers with splendid treasures and letters to king Khosrov to request peace in a most solicitous manner" (p. 66).

Not exactly on the other side but striving really hard to make the case is Engelbert Winter and Beate Dignas, *Rom und das Perserreich: Zwei Weltmächte zwischen Konfrontation und Koexistenz* (Berlin: Akademie Verlag, 2001), which depicts the two as rival superpowers, not inappropriately.

Given that there is only one comprehensive modern history in English, *Heraclius: Emperor of Byzantium* (Cambridge: Cambridge University Press, 2002), it is fortunate that its author is Walter E. Kaegi Jr., an eminent Byzantinist and an eminent defender of military historiography, whose reconstruction of the course of events from shards and fragments never steps beyond the evidence.

NOTES

1. Theophanes, *Chronographia* 302–03 (AM 6113), in trans. Cyril Mango and Roger Scott, *The Chronicle of Theophanes Confessor: Byzantine and Near Eastern History, AD 284–813* (Oxford: Clarendon Press, 1997).

2. Theophanes, *Chronographia* 303–4 (AM 6113).

3. Theophanes, *Chronographia* 303–4 (AM 6113).

4. Heraclius, *Chronicon Paschale* p. 709, in trans. Michael Whitby and Mary Whitby, *Chronicon Paschale 284–628 AD* (Liverpool: Liverpool University Press, 1989).

5. *The Armenian History Attributed to Sebeos* 123, in trans. R. W. Thomson (Liverpool: Liverpool University Press, 1999).

6. Heraclius, *Chronicon Paschale* p. 718.

7. Theophanes, *Chronographia* 315 (AM 6117).

8. Menander Protector, *History* fragment 10.3, in trans. R. C. Blockley, *The History of Menander the Guardsman* (Liverpool: Francis Cairns, 1985).

9. *Armenian History* 126.

10. Theophanes, *Chronographia* 324 (AM 6118).

4

GUSTAVUS ADOLPHUS AND THE RISE OF SWEDEN

Peter R. Mansoor

The rise of Sweden in the seventeenth century is one of the singular moments in the history of great power relations. At the turn of the seventeenth century, Sweden was a local power limited to its homeland in the Nordic region and hemmed in by Denmark, Poland, and Russia. This situation changed due in large measure to the leadership of the warrior king Gustavus Adolphus and his capable chancellor, Axel Oxenstierna. Gustavus harnessed an ongoing revolution in military affairs to make the Swedish army the most lethal and effective in Europe. He used that force to turn the tide of a conflict that had gone badly for his coreligionists in Germany and to transform the Baltic Sea into a Swedish lake. Gustavus for a time exemplified the great man theory of history, the idea that one can explain history primarily through the lens of unique and powerful individuals who shape the course of human events through their superior abilities. But Sweden's decline in the early eighteenth century validated the importance of more systematic limitations on power: population, economic strength, geography, and resources, among others.

THE WARRIOR KING

When Gustavus ascended the throne in 1611 at the age of seventeen after the death of his father, Charles IX, Sweden was hardly a candidate for great power status. The young king "found the

crown and the inhabitants of Sweden equally impoverished."[1]
The Swedish population of one and a quarter million was dwarfed
by that of continental Europe. Swedish farms could barely feed
this many, causing one contemporary statesman to remark, "The
Swedes are a hungry people, and hence they are dangerous and
hard-hearted."[2] Ninety percent of Swedes were peasants, mean-
ing that economic inequality was less pronounced than in other
European nations of the time.[3] During Gustavus's reign Sweden
did not suffer the types of revolts and civil wars that racked other
contemporary polities.[4] And although the Swedish peasants may
or may not have actually been "dangerous and hard-hearted,"

they most certainly were the material from which effective armies
are made.

Gustavus, although intelligent and broadly educated in the
classics, languages (he eventually spoke Greek, Latin, Dutch, Italian, Russian, and Polish in addition to his native Swedish), law,
history, theology, and the military art, confronted a situation upon
ascending the throne that would have tested the mettle of any
leader. Not only was Sweden losing its war with Denmark (the
Kalmar War, 1611–13), but Gustavus was immediately thrust into
a constitutional crisis.[5] To stabilize the realm he acceded to the
Charter of Accession that increased the power of the Swedish
nobility at the king's expense. The nobility dominated the Council of State, while the Riksdag, composed of the nobility, clergy,
burghers, and freeholders, could (and did) limit taxation.[6] But by
coming to terms with the Swedish elite, Gustavus ensured a stable
body politic that in turn supported him throughout his reign. Stability at home was essential; otherwise, as Michael Roberts, the
foremost English historian of Sweden, writes, "the emergence
of Sweden as a great power would scarcely have been conceivable."[7] Gustavus achieved that rare commodity of governance—
a "national consensus" on the aims of Swedish policy, without
which "the sacrifices which his policies demanded would scarcely
have been tolerable to his people."[8]

Gustavus was a respected and accessible monarch, admired by
and popular with his countrymen. He ruled by force of persua-
sion as much as by divine right, although he believed he was ful-
filling God's will through his actions. On this account, the Swedish people agreed with him. "Certainly one of the things which
made it easier to pursue the path of empire was the fact that
Swedish society was unusually solid and stable," writes Roberts.
"It was bound firmly together by the tough cement of the Swedish
church; it enjoyed the rare blessing of total religious unity. Sweden was the Lutheran Spain."[9]

Gustavus was a man of immense energy, but he also possessed a quick temper that sometimes made for impulsive
decision-making. The "dynamic and impetuous" Gustavus was

balanced by a calm and intellectual chancellor, Axel Oxenstierna, the two forming a remarkably close partnership that made for effective governance.[10] Administrative reforms under Gustavus and Oxenstierna created a foundation for efficient and relatively corruption-free governance. They reformed the justice system and reorganized the treasury. For the first time in its history Sweden had centralized accounting and audits, enabling systemic fiscal planning.[11] They created a College of War, an organization filled with professionals who attended to the logistical needs of the Swedish army.[12] Gustavus also reformed the Swedish system of higher education, the products of which would staff the new civil service with promotions based on merit. Within two decades "education became a powerful agent of social mobility" and with it, the rise of a meritocracy that administered effective governance through the Swedish Empire.[13] "Without some such transformation of government," writes Roberts, "the emergence of Sweden as a great power could hardly have taken place."[14]

Gustavus and Oxenstierna ended costly wars with Denmark (Kalmar War, 1611–13) and Russia (Ingrian War, 1610–17); in the former conflict they cut their losses, while in the latter they gained terms favorable to the growth of Swedish power in the Baltic region.[15] Peace enabled the Swedish leaders to focus on internal reforms and not coincidentally gave Gustavus the time to marry.[16] Revised taxes based on a new census and improved accounting stabilized state finances. Production of copper and iron ore expanded greatly, the two metals forming the basis for Swedish trade and access to credit.[17] Increased economic wherewithal and consistent tax revenues helped to establish the foundation for Swedish military power. Despite these innovations, the needs of Sweden's military forces imposed on the Swedish people a grinding tax burden, the proceeds of which were still not enough to pay for Gustavus's strategic ambitions.[18]

Gustavus oversaw the development of a domestic arms-manufacturing industry, which made Sweden self-sufficient in the production of artillery and firearms and turned it into one of the great arms-manufacturing centers of Europe.[19] He also experimented with new firearm designs, equipping his infantry with a lighter, more reliable wheel lock musket and paper cartridges, enabling the musketeers to more quickly load and fire their weapons.[20] Exports of metals and armaments were profitable; despite the rigors of wartime finances, Sweden grew richer during his reign.[21]

Gustavus compensated for the nation's lack of monetary resources by enacting a system of conscription to sustain the manpower needs of Swedish armies.[22] Conscripts were less expensive to field than mercenaries, served out of a sense of obligation, and were more obedient. The knock against them was they made poor soldiers, but that defect could (and would) be remedied by better training and leadership.[23] Gustavus personally drafted Articles of War that instituted in Swedish forces a high standard of discipline, modeled after that of the ancient Romans, both on and off the battlefield.[24] Equally importantly, he demanded that his soldiers, native-born as well as mercenaries, train extensively on the drill and maneuvers necessary to prevail in combat, and dig fortifications when they were ordered to do so.[25]

THE LINEAR WARFARE REVOLUTION IN MILITARY AFFAIRS

But economic, financial, industrial, and personnel reforms alone were insufficient to account for Sweden's rise to great power status, which would not have happened without the harnessing of an ongoing revolution in military affairs.[26] To understand the revolutionary nature of Gustavus's reforms, one must understand what they replaced. The foremost military formation of the late sixteenth and early seventeenth centuries was the tercio, a block of pikemen and musketeers thirty to forty ranks deep that lumbered into battle not unlike the phalanxes of the ancient world.[27] Cavalry charged forward only to dance the caracole, a tactic whereby succeeding horsemen would discharge their pistols at the enemy and then move to the rear to reload. The tactic negated the shock effect of cavalry charges that could decisively affect the outcome of battle.[28]

The Dutch were the first to experiment with new organizations and tactics. Maurice of Nassau pioneered linear infantry formations in the 1590s and his cousin, Count John, published a drill manual that quickly became a best seller.[29] Maurice went back to ancient Roman military writers to relearn the importance of drill and discipline, qualities sorely lacking in most contemporary military forces.[30] Smaller, linear formations required more officers and noncommissioned officers to command and control them, additional training for more complicated maneuvers, and greater discipline in the ranks.[31] Within a few years, firepower weapons replaced the blade as the signature weapon of Dutch infantry. But the Dutch were on the strategic defensive for most of their war with Spain, and thus were unable to take full advantage of the new tactics and techniques. This honor would fall to Gustavus and the Swedish army.

War was a stern teacher; by the time of Sweden's entry into the Thirty Years' War in 1630, Gustavus had spent nine years on campaign against Denmark, Russia, and Poland. Gustavus did not just learn the art of war; he mastered it. He learned the technical and tactical aspects of every branch and arm, excelled at the operational art, and was a competent strategist. His one failing was his "impetuous courage," a quality that would end his life in 1632 at the Battle of Lützen. He constantly ventured too far in front of his army on reconnaissance and was usually to be found where the action was most intense. When his men warned him of the dangers of being so constantly exposed, Gustavus would merely state, "I shall die when God wills it."[32] His intellectual curiosity, combined with his understanding of technical matters and weaponry, provided him the foundation to modify the organization and doctrine of the Swedish army to make it the premier fighting force of his day in Europe.[33]

Gustavus fashioned an army that took advantage of new technologies—matchlock muskets and mobile field artillery—to give

Swedish formations greater firepower with which to blow holes in the lumbering tercios. He furthered the reforms of the Dutch military leader Maurice of Nassau by lengthening his infantry formations, reducing their depth to just three ranks, increasing the numbers of firearms in relation to pikes, and training his soldiers to fire in volleys. By 1630 Swedish infantry regiments contained just over a thousand soldiers; these formations were only one-third to one-half the size of their Holy Roman Imperial counterparts, increasing the leader-to-led ratio and making them more maneuverable on the battlefield.[34] Gustavus also clothed his soldiers in uniforms, which helped to instill regimentation and discipline in the ranks—one of his many contributions to the art of war.[35]

An expert gunner himself, Gustavus could credibly claim the title of creator of field artillery. Under his reforms every Swedish infantry regiment received two light three-pounder guns, each capable of being moved by a single horse, to augment its firepower.[36] Gustavus drilled his army in offensive as well as defensive marching techniques, and reformed his cavalry to restore shock action to the battlefield by eliminating the clumsy caracole in favor of charges by horsemen equipped with swords.[37] Musketeer detachments supported the cavalry, giving the horsemen even greater firepower. These organizational reforms capitalized on new technologies to create world-class military formations that dominated the battlefields of central Europe from 1630 to 1648.[38] Through his harnessing of this revolution in military affairs (RMA), Gustavus transformed Sweden "from a defeated and humiliated minor power to one with the capacity to dominate the Baltic by the mid-seventeenth century."[39]

The excellent Swedish army would have been pedestrian had it not been commanded by superior leaders, and Sweden was blessed during the period of its ascendancy with "commanders of exceptional quality."[40] Gustavus was what Carl von Clausewitz would term a military genius: well educated in the military art, technically proficient in the arms of his day, a master trainer, personally courageous, respected by all ranks, and audacious in battle.[41] He sought battles of annihilation in an era dominated by siege warfare. Napoleon, another military genius who strode the

European stage 150 years later, "included Gustavus in the small band—not more than six or seven in all—of the commanders whom he considered to be truly great."[42]

Gustavus learned the art of war through both reading and practical experience, primarily in wars to protect his dynastic inheritance against his cousin Sigismund III of Poland, who coveted the Swedish throne that he had once held.[43] Gustavus spent a good portion of the 1620s improving Sweden's position vis-à-vis its strategic competitors in the Baltic region. Under Gustavus's watchful eye Sweden developed a navy of thirty-one warships and numerous transports that both guarded the homeland and provided a bridge to transport Swedish armies across the Baltic Sea.[44] The gains of this decade, including the seizure of Riga, dominance over Polish and Prussian ports along the Baltic coast, and a favorable agreement with Denmark that reaffirmed the principle of free trade for Swedish vessels, were substantial.[45] After several years of hostilities with Poland, the Truce of Altmark (1629) gave Sweden the right for six years to two-thirds of shipping tolls at ports in the Polish-Lithuanian Commonwealth and Prussia, and cleared the way—both politically and financially—for Swedish intervention in ongoing hostilities in Germany.[46]

The RMA Gustavus honed was not just the creation of linear formations, but the development of combined-arms warfare in which infantry, cavalry, and artillery worked in close concert on the battlefield rather than engaging in separate fights. By 1630 Gustavus had designed formations that made best use of the gunpowder and blade weapons of his day. Mobility, firepower, and shock action were the hallmarks of Swedish forces.[47] He had perfected his army and its military doctrine in the Polish wars; he would now use it to dominate the battlefields of Germany.

THE THIRTY YEARS' WAR

The Thirty Years' War was a calamity for early modern Europe, but its resolution paved the way for the birth of the modern state system. Its origins are complex, with dynastic squabbles, religion, international power politics, social tensions, climate change, and other factors interwoven together. Upwards of 30 to 40 percent of the population of Germany died in the conflict, making it the deadliest era on a per capita basis in central European history.

The war began in 1618 with a local revolt in Bohemia; it then spiraled out of control as great powers intervened, thereby internationalizing the conflict. Hostilities created a level of devastation in central Europe that none of the major powers could have imagined when the war began. Bohemian forces made it as far as the gates of Vienna in November 1619, but lacking a siege train and crippled by a dearth of supplies, they retreated as winter neared. Hapsburg armies, bolstered by financial support from Spain and the papacy and military support from Bavaria and Saxony, then crushed the rebellion in Bohemia and Upper and Lower Austria by force, ending it for good after winning the decisive Battle of White Mountain on a prominence overlooking Prague on November 8, 1620.[48]

In the ensuing three years Imperial and Spanish armies proceeded to carve up the Palatinate, home of the would-be king of Bohemia, Frederick V. After a decisive victory by the Imperial army commanded by Johann Tserclaes, Count of Tilly, at the Battle of Stadtlohn on August 6, 1623, and the subsequent demobilization of Protestant forces in East Frisia in January 1624, the war appeared to be over. Holy Roman Emperor Ferdinand II reimposed the Catholic religion on the conquered territories, shutting Protestants out of economic and political power. Many nobles converted to retain their status, while punitive measures drove others, especially those of lesser means, into exile.[49]

The triumph was short-lived, as Ferdinand's victory and subsequent program of re-Catholicization provoked a backlash. Imperial victories; the duplicitous diplomacy of England, the United Provinces (the Dutch Republic), and the Palatinate; and the potential for the intervention of strategic rival Sweden worried Christian IV of Denmark. In 1625 he sought to defend his strategic position in the Baltic and his dynastic interests in Lower Saxony by mobilizing an army and directing it against the forces of the Catholic League of the Holy Roman Empire. He browbeat the Lower Saxons into giving him control over their forces. His assembled army, buoyed at the end of the year by English and Dutch subsidies, was joined over the course of the next year by German, Dutch, French, English, and Scottish mercenaries.[50]

Ferdinand had by this time turned to Count Albrecht von Wallenstein, a relatively junior nobleman who had risen by amassing great wealth via confiscated Protestant estates (and using it to curry favor with the Emperor), to raise an army to complement (and rival) the Catholic League forces commanded by Count Tilly. Faced with the threat from Denmark, Wallenstein raised upwards of one hundred thousand men, although his field army numbered considerably fewer given the need to garrison various base areas.[51] He and Tilly used their armies to hammer the Danish forces and their mercenary allies, winning victories in 1626 at the battles of Dessau Bridge and Lutter, and destroying the army commanded by Ernst Graf von Mansfeld. Christian's fortunes proved no better in 1627, as Wallenstein and Tilly overran the province of Holstein and forced his army back into the islands of the Danish Archipelago. Emperor Ferdinand rewarded Wallenstein by assigning him the duchy of Mecklenburg and the bishopric of Schwerin, deposing in the process the two former dukes who had supported Christian with troops.[52]

Wallenstein was unable to build a navy to compete with Christian's sea power, while the Danish monarch was able to restore the strength of his army by extending conscription to Norway. Over the course of 1628 Wallenstein repelled Danish raids on the mainland, compelling Christian to enter into negotiations. Christian agreed to abandon Lower Saxony in exchange for the return of Danish provinces on the mainland. Protestant fortunes dwindled as Ferdinand and the Empire appeared to be once again triumphant.[53]

Ferdinand and his advisors now came down with a severe case of victory disease. Believing their triumphs a sign of divine favor, the Emperor issued the Edict of Restitution on March 6, 1629, turning the conflict into a religious struggle for supremacy in central Europe. Many Protestant leaders decried the seizure of former Catholic lands that had been in their control for seventy years or more and were worried that the edict was just the tip of the iceberg, the beginning of a reconquest that would go hand in hand with the ongoing program of re-Catholicization.[54] The edict empowered the radicals in both Protestant and Catholic camps, leading Europe deeper into the abyss of war. Feeling newly empowered, Ferdinand also dismissed Wallenstein, the subject of a public smear campaign by jealous rivals, as commander of the Imperial army in the late summer of 1630, the command falling to Tilly.[55]

The guiding hand behind the opposition to Ferdinand was now the principal minister of another Catholic nation, Cardinal Richelieu of France, who feared Spanish encirclement and Hapsburg power more than he did Protestant rebels.[56] Once Imperial forces defeated the Danes, Richelieu searched for a counter to Hapsburg might in central Europe. Sweden fit the bill. The French alliance gave Gustavus diplomatic cover and what he needed most—money, to the tune of 400,000 reichsthalers per year.[57] The subsidy was not enough to buy Gustavus's undying loyalty, but given the state of Swedish finances in 1630, every bit helped.

Gustavus viewed the war on the continent with trepidation. Imperial victories over his strategic competitor, Christian of Denmark; the arrival of Wallenstein's forces on the shores of the Baltic; and the creation of an Imperial navy turned northern Germany into a major national-security priority for Gustavus and Sweden.[58] Swedish troops arrived in Stralsund, a Germanic harbor on the Baltic Sea, in June 1628 to help the Danes secure the city against Wallenstein's forces. The burghers decided the Swedish garrison could stay to protect the city against further danger, and Stralsund quickly became a Swedish protectorate. The agreement was a strategic coup, as Stralsund provided Gustavus and the Swedes a beachhead across the Baltic Sea, one that Sweden would hold for nearly two centuries.[59]

SWEDISH INTERVENTION

Sweden's intervention in the Thirty Years' War occurred primarily out of fear of Imperial domination of the Baltic coast. Despite the hopes of Protestant militants that Gustavus had come to save them and reverse the hated Edict of Restitution, the Swedish king was intent on more secular aims, the most important of which was reducing the threat to Sweden caused by the buildup of Imperial power in northern Germany.[60]

In July 1630 the Swedish army deployed across the Baltic Sea in two hundred transports and ships of the line, with ninety-two infantry companies, 116 companies of cavalry, and an extensive artillery train.[61] More reinforcements and local recruits brought the expeditionary force up to twenty-nine thousand men by November.[62] The Swedish army was powerful and technically and tactically gifted, but untested outside of the Polish theater. Gustavus also lacked the funds to sustain it for an extended campaign in Germany. But he enjoyed a number of advantages that previous combatants in Germany lacked: "He commanded a disciplined and experienced army; he ruled over an orderly and loyal country; he possessed important reserves of war material— particularly iron and copper."[63]

What Gustavus needed most was allies in Germany, but most German rulers remained wary of siding with the unproven Swedish king. Gustavus compelled Duke Bogislaw XIV of Pomerania to enter into an alliance by marching a portion of his army into Stettin. Christian Wilhelm of Magdeburg more willingly declared for Gustavus on July 27, 1630.[64] Tilly sent Count Gottfried Heinrich Pappenheim with several thousand troops to cordon off Magdeburg, and a proper siege began the following spring when Tilly arrived with his army. Gustavus attempted to deflect Tilly's attention by storming Frankfurt an der Oder and seizing Landsberg, but the Catholic commander remained unmoved. After Magdeburg's defenders refused Tilly's proposals for the city's surrender, Imperial forces stormed the city on

May 20, 1631. Fire destroyed 90 percent of Magdeburg's buildings and Imperial troops committed a number of atrocities, while fully two-thirds of the city's thirty thousand civilians and defenders died in the carnage.[65] One citizen, describing the slaughter, wrote, "Through such enduring fury—which laid this great, magnificent city, which had been like a princess in the entire land, into complete burning embers and put it into such enormous misery and unspeakable need and heartache—many thousands of innocent men, women, and children were, with horrid, fearful screams of pain and alarm, miserably murdered and wretchedly executed in manifold ways, so that no words can sufficiently describe it, nor tears bemoan it."[66] Pappenheim was unfazed, writing, "I believe that over twenty thousand souls were lost. It is certain that no more terrible work and divine punishment has been seen since the Destruction of Jerusalem. All of our soldiers became rich. God with us."[67]

Protestant leaders lambasted Gustavus for his failure to relieve Magdeburg.[68] Tilly and other Imperial forces now moved to crush other Protestant militants, but the destruction of Magdeburg galvanized resistance. Protestant leaders used the Sack of Magdeburg as propaganda to convince their followers to side with the Swedish king.[69] The United Provinces promised subsidies for the Swedish army. Gustavus marched on Berlin and forced his brother-in-law, Elector Georg Wilhelm, to cede Spandau and Küstrin and support his forces with regular contributions amounting to 30,000 reichsthalers per month.[70] Landgrave Wilhelm V of Hessen-Kassel declared for Sweden on July 27. Gustavus furthered his cause by inflicting a stinging defeat on Tilly's army at Werben on August 1.[71]

THE BATTLE OF BREITENFELD

Gustavus received a further boost to his support base when Elector Johann Georg of Saxony, faced with an invasion by Tilly's army, declared for Sweden on September 12.[72] Saxony was a rich prize;

it had yet to be ravaged by war and possessed valuable resources as well as a large, albeit poorly trained, army. The Swedes quickly marched south to join up with the Saxon army near Leipzig. The two armies together numbered thirty-nine thousand men— twenty-three thousand Swedish (and mercenaries) and sixteen thousand Saxons—with fifty-one guns in the excellent Swedish artillery train and additional batteries of mobile three-pounder field artillery pieces that supported each infantry regiment.[73]

Both sides now sought battle: Gustavus to convince Germany's Protestants to side with him; Tilly to suppress growing Protestant disaffection. The two sides met on a broad plain near the village of Breitenfeld on September 17, 1631. Tilly was slightly outmanned, his army numbering thirty-one thousand men and twenty-seven guns.[74]

The battle commenced at midday with a two-hour artillery cannonade, with the seventeen Imperial tercios taking the worst of the barrage. Pappenheim then impetuously attacked the Swedish right wing, commanded by General Johan Banér, but the Swedish cavalry and interspersed musketeers repulsed seven charges. On the other side of the battlefield, Catholic League and Croat cavalry bore down on the inexperienced Saxons on the left side of the Swedish line; the Saxons broke and fled after some initial resistance. The Imperial cavalry took off in pursuit of the Saxons and stopped only to loot the Swedish baggage trains, while Tilly maneuvered his tercios obliquely to the east to exploit the Saxon departure from the battlefield.

On most battlefields and against most armies of the time, the flight of the Saxons and the uncovering of the Swedish left flank would have decided the outcome. But not on this battlefield and not against the reformed Swedish army. Swedish general Gustav Karlsson Horn deftly maneuvered his reserves to plug the hole left by the retreating Saxon forces, while the Swedish brigades countered with musket and light artillery firepower that decimated the densely packed Imperial formations. Shouting "God with us!" Gustavus and Banér then led the Swedish cavalry in a rout of Pappenheim's exhausted troopers, enveloped the Imperial left flank, seized the relatively immobile enemy artillery train, and bore down on the overstretched Imperial infantry. The Imperial tercios eventually broke from the battering they took from the Swedish guns. The setting sun witnessed the collapse of the Imperial army, with 7,600 dead on the battlefield, another nine thousand taken prisoner, and thousands more wounded, including its commander. By contrast, the Swedes only lost 2,100 men. Tilly was only able to rally thirteen thousand survivors after the battle, while Gustavus was able to replenish his ranks by enlisting captured Imperial troops into his army.[75]

In one afternoon, the balance of power in central Europe had shifted decisively in favor of Gustavus and his Protestant allies, a contingency made possible by the harnessing of a revolution in military affairs on behalf of Swedish power. The scale of the triumph at Breitenfeld stunned even Gustavus, who now was faced with the enviable task of exploiting his victory. He had achieved his immediate aim of securing the Baltic coast, but "had made no contingency plans for a victory on this scale—indeed, he did not even possess any detailed maps covering the lands south of Brandenburg or west of Magdeburg."[76]

Gustavus and his army advanced to the southwest through Thuringia to seize Erfurt, Würzburg, Frankfurt am Main, Mainz, and Heidelberg, while another Swedish force seized Mecklenburg. Before the end of the year Bremen declared for Sweden, strengthening Gustavus's increasingly firm grip on the Baltic coast.

MAKING WAR PAY FOR WAR

Sweden's resources were in themselves insufficient for war making on the scale of Gustavus's campaigns in Germany. His solution was to make war pay for itself. If Sweden lacked the necessary resources for war, it would acquire them on the continent. Contributions from allied and conquered territories, subsidies provided by France and the United Provinces, and duties collected at Baltic ports multiplied the monetary assets at Sweden's disposal tenfold.[77] In the first four years of their intervention in Germany, the Swedes spent 5.5 million riksdalers of their own money, garnered another 3.7 million reichsthalers in tolls from Polish and Prussian ports, and received more than 1 million reichsthalers in French subsidies. This collateral enabled the Swedes to borrow money from financiers in Hamburg and Amsterdam.[78]

Despite these sources of income, fully two-thirds of Sweden's war expenses had to come from monetary contributions exacted on German communities (either systematically collected from occupied territories or as ransom paid by captured towns to avoid plunder) and exactions in kind for food, fodder, and lodging. In this regard Gustavus's treatment of German territories differed little from Wallenstein's, albeit the Swedish troops were much more disciplined in their relations with local communities.[79] Although Gustavus's expectations exceeded the capacity of most communities to pay, he nevertheless gained a great deal of income from them. "German money not only paid the mercenaries who comprised between three-quarters and nine-tenths of the total army, but also covered 51 per cent of the 1 million riksdalers spent on the Swedish and Finnish contingent each year between 1630 and 1648."[80] With Swedish arms ascendant and the system of contributions in place, "after 1630 the war practically financed itself."[81]

Despite its successes, the system of contributions that shifted the financial burden for war onto German communities had one fatal drawback: it required victories to sustain the contributions. "As long as Sweden continued to win victories she could count on winning them at little cost to herself," writes Michael Roberts. "Retreat and defeat upset the financial equation. Peace destroyed it."[82]

As disease and combat took their toll, Gustavus also required local sources of manpower to replenish his ranks. Nearly half of the initial contingent that landed on the continent in the summer of 1630 died by the end of the year (mostly by disease); by the end of 1631, Gustavus had lost fifty thousand men. Of course, not all of the casualties were Swedes and Finns, but the grim reaper's toll was nonetheless steep. The life expectancy of a Swedish conscript in Germany after joining the force was just four years. In the words of a noted historian of the Thirty Years' War, in Sweden "whole villages became depopulated of young men, for a conscription order was virtually a sentence of death."[83] German manpower made up the shortfall as the Swedish campaign in Germany continued. At Breitenfeld and Lützen, Swedish soldiers accounted for no more than 20 percent of Gustavus's army, although they were the indispensable core of his forces.[84] With German additions to the order of battle, Swedish strength in Germany peaked at 140,000 men in mid-1632.[85]

THE EMPIRE STRIKES BACK

Breitenfeld and subsequent Swedish advances threw the Catholic states of central Europe into a panic. Most saw no other recourse than to support Ferdinand and continue the fight.[86] With Tilly mortally wounded at the Battle of the Lech, the Emperor recalled Wallenstein on April 13, 1632, and gave him extensive powers that clearly made him the most powerful commander in the Empire.[87] Wallenstein gathered sixty-five thousand men and reformed the Imperial army, halving the depth of the clumsy tercios and adopting other tactical innovations, such as volley fire and light field artillery, which put his forces more on a par with the Swedes.[88]

Swedish power in Germany reached its high mark in 1632. In that year Swedish forces fought the Imperial army and its allies in four major battles, culminating in the Battle of Lützen. Fighting in the spring and summer of 1632 focused on Bavaria, with Imperial armies winning battles at Fürth and Nuremberg (Alte Veste) and Swedish forces triumphant at Rain (Lech River). Bavaria, which before 1632 had been spared the ravages of war, lay in ruins, its capital city of Munich in Swedish hands. Disease and privation hit people and animals on both sides hard. During the siege of Nuremberg, twenty-nine thousand people died of various causes.[89] By mid-September less than half of the Swedish cavalry remained mounted, while on the Imperial side Wallenstein had to abandon one thousand wagonloads of supplies for lack of horses to haul them.[90]

In the fall of 1632 Wallenstein marched on Saxony in an attempt to pressure Gustavus's major ally and winter on its territory. Gustavus rushed north in response, searching for an opportunity to deal the Imperial army another thrashing on the scale of Breitenfeld. The two armies met on the plain east of the small village of Lützen. Gustavus attacked with twelve thousand eight hundred infantry, six thousand two hundred cavalry, twenty heavy cannon, and forty regimental guns, while Wallenstein defended with eight thousand infantry, eight thousand cavalry, and twenty-four heavy guns.[91] After waiting for a dense fog to lift, Gustavus began the action by leading his cavalry to rout the small contingent of Croat horsemen on the Imperial left flank; but Swedish infantry, attacking into the center of the Imperial formations, made little headway. Pappenheim, having received a recall order from Wallenstein, arrived in the nick of time in the early afternoon with two thousand three hundred cavalry after a forced march of more than twenty miles. Together with the reformed Croat contingent, Pappenheim drove the Swedish cavalry back. Both he and Gustavus were killed in the confused fighting, after which the Swedish infantry fought with a fury borne of vengeance for their slain king. By the end of the day, Wallenstein had lost at least six thousand men along with his entire artillery train. Swedish forces held the battlefield, but having suffered six thousand casualties of their own as well as the loss of their king, the victory was tactically hollow—and strategically disastrous.[92]

Gustavus's death at Lützen restored strategic equilibrium in the war. Oxenstierna assumed the leadership of the Swedish war effort and worked to extricate his nation from the conflict, but it proved far easier to enter the war than to leave it with Swedish goals intact. Sweden looked to France for help, while the Empire sought Spanish assistance. The war, which to this point was primarily a civil conflict within the Empire, was about to become a regional conflict involving most of the great powers of Europe. The death of Gustavus, seen by many contemporaries as the champion of Protestantism, had squeezed the last idealistic element out of the equation. European powers would wage war henceforth more out of fear and interest than for honor, with "politics emptied of faith."[93] The Imperial recovery that followed the Battle of Lützen confirms what history has repeatedly shown: The half-life of a revolution in military affairs in a conflict between peer competitors is fairly short. Theodore Ayrault Dodge, a military historian writing in the nineteenth century, states, "His [Gustavus's] victories showed the superiority of his system so thoroughly that the whole world turned from the ancient methods to study what he had introduced."[94] Historian Geoffrey Parker makes a similar observation: "Already at Lützen, in November 1632, the Imperialists (under Albrecht von Wallenstein) had thinned out their lines, perfected volley firing, and added field artillery. After this, most other states began to acquire large numbers of Swedish guns—up to 1,000 a year were being exported by the 1650s, mostly for sale in Amsterdam—and the musket remained the 'queen of the battlefield' for over two centuries."[95]

Sweden now had to contend with Imperial armies organized much like its own. Given its sudden lack of military superiority, the Swedes needed allies. Under Chancellor Oxenstierna's leadership, Sweden's goals were to retain control of the Baltic coast while securing alliances with Protestant leaders in central Germany to serve as a buffer against the Empire.[96] He was the driving force behind the creation of the Protestant Heilbronn League (formed in April 1633), a defensive alliance responsible for a collective army that would ensure the demands of the alliance's members were met—by force if necessary. These included "respect for the principles and constitution of the Holy Roman Empire," the rescinding of the Edict of Restitution, and Swedish control of Pomerania and the Baltic coast.[97]

Financing the army was easier said than done, especially because of the large amount of back pay owed to the soldiers. To satisfy their demands, the soldiers in southern Germany took a common course of action in early modern Europe—they mutinied. Along with other measures, League leaders resorted to plunder to meet the needs of the moment. The mutinies died down by late summer, but the campaign season was slipping away. Wallenstein's victory over a Swedish force at Steinau on September 27 led to the surrender of eight thousand men and the loss of Silesia. Pressure on the Swedes was only temporarily lifted by the assassination of Wallenstein on February 25, 1634, in clouded circumstances.[98]

After Imperial and Spanish forces decisively defeated the Swedish army at the Battle of Nordlingen in September 1634, the Swedish position in southern Germany crumbled and the Heilbronn League collapsed.[99] Swedish forces withdrew to Mecklenburg and Pomerania to lick their wounds. Oxenstierna attempted to execute a common strategy of a great power caught in a wartime morass—the use of proxies to do the fighting for Sweden. "The Polish war is our war; win or lose, it is our gain or loss," he wrote the Swedish Council of State on January 7, 1635. "This German war, I don't know what it is, only that we pour out blood here for the sake of reputation, and have naught but ingratitude to expect. . . . We must let this German business be left to the Germans, who will be the only people to get any good of it (if there is any), and therefore not spend any more men or money here, but rather try by all means to wriggle out of it."[100]

But after Nordlingen, most of Sweden's allies in Germany deserted. German Protestant leaders signed the Treaty of Prague on May 30, 1635, which effectively rescinded the Edict of Restitution and granted a general amnesty in return for the dissolution of the Catholic League and the Protestant Heilbronn League. As part of the Treaty, individual states within the Empire were prohibited from entering into foreign alliances, a measure clearly aimed at both Sweden and France.[101]

THE RETURN OF THE SWEDES

Until 1635 German states had fought the war with some foreign assistance, but afterward foreign states dominated the battle space. The ink was not even dry on the Treaty of Prague when France, now bereft of allies with which to counter Imperial and Spanish strength, declared war. Sweden was down but not out; with the aid of French intervention and subsidies, Swedish armies recovered and won battles at Wittstock (1636), Breitenfeld again (1642), Jankov (1645), Allerheim (1645), and Zusmarshausen (1648). In 1643 and 1644 Swedish armies crushed Danish resistance in Verden, Bremen, and the Jutland peninsula. Shortly thereafter (April 1645), the Swedes reached the gates of Vienna, only to be turned back when their Transylvanian allies deserted them. Despite this setback, by the end of 1645 Swedish military power once again reigned supreme in Germany.[102] The Emperor's German allies deserted him one by one. Plague and global cooling, which substantially reduced harvests in the late 1640s, made the endgame truly horrific. By the end of the war in 1648, Germany had lost 40 percent of its rural and a third of its urban population.[103]

The subsequent Peace of Westphalia worked to Sweden's advantage. The resolution ensured a fragmented Germany, preventing the Empire from contesting Swedish control of the Baltic region. Sweden received the western half of Pomerania, Wismar, Verden, and Bremen as well as a large indemnity to pay off (demobilize) its army.[104] Sweden had emerged as a major actor in European affairs and it played a key role in the resolution of the conflict at the Westphalia Congress. Through judicious reforms and brilliant leadership, Gustavus Adolphus and his chancellor had transformed a resource-poor, geographically challenged state into a military juggernaut. The wise and judicious leadership of Chancellor Oxenstierna sustained Sweden's position even after the great king's death.

CONCLUSION

Swedish dominance would not outlast the reign of Charles XII (1697–1718), who pursued military victory over more powerful neighbors at the expense of wise policy and sound strategy. In the end the "inexorable facts of the geopolitical situation" doomed the Swedish Empire.[105] Gustavus had leveraged a revolution in military affairs to transform Sweden into a great power, but this development could not ensure the state's lasting prominence in international affairs. Revolutions in military affairs have a limited shelf life, after which other components of national power lend their considerable weight to the balance between states. Gustavus played a mediocre hand incredibly well, but the inability to transfer his genius to his successors eventually sealed the fate of the Swedish Empire. After the Swedish collapse, Russia and Germany would henceforth dominate the Baltic region.

If we can learn anything from the experience of Gustavus Adolphus and Sweden in the seventeenth century, it would be that superb leadership and superior military forces can make a difference in international affairs—for a time. But inspired leadership is not a substitute for an effective national-security apparatus for crafting sound policy and strategy and applying the full range of state power to achieve desired goals. Military force, especially with innovative doctrine, organization, and equipment, can be incredibly effective if employed in accordance with a broader grand strategy. Alone it is a blunt instrument; at times effective at destruction, but incapable by itself of stabilizing populations and territory in the absence of a political settlement crafted under the aegis of a legitimate international order. Such a settlement eluded Gustavus. After his death in battle, Germany would suffer for another decade and a half before the Peace of Westphalia brought a measure of stability to Europe, but only after the horrors of war finally cooled the passions of religious partisanship and made the state the ultimate arbiter of the use of violence for political ends.

RECOMMENDATIONS FOR FURTHER READING

The remarkable life of Gustavus Adolphus and his role in the rise of Sweden has spawned a rich historical literature. Many of the early works stressed his role as the champion of Protestantism, which, of course, was not the primary motivation for Sweden's wars on the European continent. More balanced treatments began to appear in the nineteenth century, although modern scholarship has surpassed these earlier works in quality if not quantity. The leading figure in modern scholarship concerning Gustavus Adolphus and the rise of Sweden is Michael Roberts, whose works span the gamut from biography to national to international history. Among his publications are a biography, *Gustavus Adolphus and the Rise of Sweden* (London: The English Universities Press, 1973); a lengthy but excellent national history, *A History of Sweden, 1611–1632* (2 vols., London, New York: Longmans, Green and Co., 1953, 1958); and a shorter work on empire, *The Swedish Imperial Experience, 1560–1718* (Cambridge: Cambridge University Press, 1979).

The military revolution in which Gustavus played an important role has also energized an extensive literature. Three works in particular stand out: Geoffrey Parker's *The Military Revolution: Military Innovation and the Rise of the West, 1500–1800*, second edition (New York: Cambridge University Press, 1996); the superb volume edited by Clifford J. Rogers, *The Military Revolution Debate: Readings on the Military Transformation of Early Modern Europe* (Boulder: Westview Press, 1995); and MacGregor Knox and Williamson Murray's volume on revolutions in military affairs, *The Dynamics of Military Revolution, 1300–2050* (Cambridge, New York: Cambridge University Press, 2001). For broader treatments of the Thirty Years' War, readers are encouraged to consult Peter H. Wilson, *The Thirty Years War: Europe's Tragedy* (Cambridge, MA: Harvard University Press, 2009), and the older but still excellent volume by Geoffrey Parker, *The Thirty Years' War*, second (revised) edition (London, New York: Routledge, 1997). Documentary histories of the Thirty Years' War include Tryntje Helfferich, *The Thirty Years War: A Documentary History* (Indianapolis: Hackett, 2009); Benjamin Marschke and Hans Medick, eds., *Experiencing the Thirty Years War: A Brief History with Documents* (Boston, New

York: Bedford/St. Martin's, 2013); and Peter H. Wilson, *The Thirty Years War: A Sourcebook* (New York: Palgrave Macmillan, 2010).

NOTES

1. John L. Stevens, *History of Gustavus Adolphus* (New York: G. P. Putnam's Sons, 1884), 94.

2. Michael Roberts, *The Swedish Imperial Experience, 1560–1718* (Cambridge: Cambridge University Press, 1979), 43.

3. Peter H. Wilson, *The Thirty Years War: Europe's Tragedy* (Cambridge: Harvard University Press, 2009), 178, cited in subsequent notes as Wilson, *Thirty Years War*.

4. Roberts, *Swedish Imperial Experience*, 65.

5. Michael Roberts, *Gustavus Adolphus and the Rise of Sweden* (London: The English Universities Press, 1973), 31.

6. Wilson, *Thirty Years War*, 181.

7. Roberts, *Gustavus Adolphus*, 34.

8. Roberts, *Gustavus Adolphus*, 39; Roberts, *Swedish Imperial Experience*, 77.

9. Roberts, *Swedish Imperial Experience*, 64.

10. Wilson, *Thirty Years War*, 183–84; Roberts, *Gustavus Adolphus*, 34; Stevens, *History*, 81.

11. Roberts, *Gustavus Adolphus*, 86.

12. Roberts, *Swedish Imperial Experience*, 56–57.

13. Roberts, *Swedish Imperial Experience*, 95; see also Stevens, *History*, 90–93.

14. Roberts, *Gustavus Adolphus*, 83.

15. Roberts, *Gustavus Adolphus*, 42–47.

16. His marriage to Maria Eleonora, sister of George William, Elector of Brandenburg, produced a daughter but little else. It did, however, focus Gustavus's attention on German matters at a time when the Empire was about to erupt into civil conflict. Roberts, *Gustavus Adolphus*, 51–53; Nils Ahnlund, *Gustav Adolf the Great*, trans. Michael Roberts (Princeton, NJ: Princeton University Press, 1940), 86.

17. Wilson, *Thirty Years War*, 185. Sweden had plentiful copper deposits and in fact enjoyed a near monopoly on copper production in Europe in the first half of the seventeenth century.

18. For an examination of the growth of the Swedish military state and war economy, see Jan Lindegren, "The Swedish 'Military State,' 1560–1720," *Scandinavian Journal of History*, 10:4 (1985): 305–27.

19. Stevens, *History*, 100.

20. Trevor N. Dupuy, *The Military Life of Gustavus Adolphus: Father of Modern War* (New York: Franklin Watts, 1969), 60; Theodore Ayrault Dodge,

Gustavus Adolphus (Boston: Houghton Mifflin, 1895; repr. Mechanicsburg, PA: Stackpole, 1996), 37.

21. Roberts, *Swedish Imperial Experience*, 49–50.

22. Geoffrey Parker, *The Thirty Years' War*, 2nd (rev.) ed. (London, New York: Routledge, 1997), 193.

23. Roberts, *Gustavus Adolphus*, 104–5.

24. William Watts, "The Swedish Discipline (1632)," in Tryntje Helfferich, ed. and trans., *The Thirty Years War: A Documentary History* (Indianapolis: Hackett, 2009), 124–37.

25. "No soldiour shall think himselfe too good to worke upon any piece of Fortification, or other place, where they shalbe commanded for our service; upon paine of punishment." Watts, "Swedish Discipline," 129.

26. Two of the foremost authorities on revolutions in military affairs describe them thus: "Military organizations embark upon an RMA by devising new ways of destroying their opponents. To do so, they must come to grips with fundamental changes in the social, political, and military landscapes; in some cases they must anticipate those changes. Revolutions in military affairs require the assembly of a complex mix of tactical, organizational, doctrinal, and technological innovations in order to implement a new conceptual approach to warfare or to a specialized sub-branch of warfare." Williamson Murray and MacGregor Knox, "Thinking about Revolutions in Warfare," in MacGregor Knox and Williamson Murray, eds., *The Dynamics of Military Revolution, 1300–2050* (Cambridge: Cambridge University Press, 2001), 12.

27. "The Pike and Shot of the Spanish Tercio," *Military History Matters*, May 11, 2011, https://www.military-history.org/articles/wmd-pike-and-shot-the-spanish-tercio.htm; Michael Roberts, *A History of Sweden, 1611–1632*, vol. 2, *1626–1632* (London, New York: Longmans, Green and Co., 1958), 173–76.

28. Roberts, *History of Sweden*, 179–80.

29. Geoffrey Parker, *The Military Revolution: Military Innovation and the Rise of the West, 1500–1800*, 2nd ed. (New York: Cambridge University Press, 1996), 20–22.

30. Parker, *Military Revolution*, 19.

31. Michael Roberts, "The Military Revolution, 1560–1660: An Inaugural Lecture Delivered before the Queen's University of Belfast," reprinted in Clifford J. Rogers, ed., *The Military Revolution Debate: Readings on the Military Transformation of Early Modern Europe* (Boulder, CO: Westview Press, 1995), 14.

32. Ahnlund, *Gustav Adolf*, 127.

33. Dupuy, *Military Life*, 54–55.

34. Benjamin Chapman, *The History of Gustavus Adolphus and of the Thirty Years' War, Up to the King's Death* (London: Longman, Brown, Green, and Longmans, 1856), 92.

35. Dodge, *Gustavus Adolphus*, 19.

36. Dodge, *Gustavus Adolphus*, 43.

37. A stout pike wall could stymie cavalry, so these charges only succeeded against opposing cavalry, disorganized troops, or against the flank or rear of an enemy formation.

38. Parker, *Military Revolution*, 23; Dodge, *Gustavus Adolphus*, 254; Roberts, "The Military Revolution," 13–35. Roberts was the first to posit the revolutionary nature of Gustavus's military system in a lecture at the Queen's University of Belfast in 1955. Since then his thesis on what he termed the "Military Revolution" of early modern Europe has undergone significant expansion and revision by others, but his discussion of Gustavus's use of the reforms of Maurice of Nassau to create the most effective army of his time is still relevant.

39. Roberts, *Gustavus Adolphus*, 107–10; Wilson, *Thirty Years War*, 187.

40. Roberts, *Gustavus Adolphus*, 112.

41. Carl von Clausewitz, *On War*, ed. and trans. Michael Howard and Peter Paret (Princeton, NJ: Princeton University Press, 1976), 100–112.

42. Roberts, *Gustavus Adolphus*, 114. Actually, there were eight generals in Napoleon's pantheon of military geniuses: Alexander, Hannibal, Julius Caesar, Gustavus Adolphus, Turenne, Prince Eugene, Frederick the Great, and himself.

43. Wilson, *Thirty Years War*, 189–90; Geoffrey Parker, *The Thirty Years' War* (London: Routledge, 1984), 69–70. Sigismund III had become king of Sweden in 1592 until deposed by his uncle Charles, Gustavus's father, in 1599.

44. Roberts, *Gustavus Adolphus*, 100.

45. Roberts, *Gustavus Adolphus*, 57–59.

46. These were not easy campaigns for Gustavus; during a reconnaissance of Polish positions near Danzig in August 1627, a Polish musketeer shot Gustavus in the shoulder, disabling the king for three months. Dupuy, *Military Life*, 40.

47. Dupuy, *Military Life*, 66.

48. Wilson, *Thirty Years War*, 294–308. The result was decisive: Bohemia would remain Catholic and under the control of the Austro-Hungarian Empire until its breakup at the end of World War I.

49. Wilson, *Thirty Years War*, 357–61.

50. Wilson, *Thirty Years War*, 391; Parker, *Thirty Years' War*, 73–74.

51. Wilson, *Thirty Years War*, 395.

52. Wilson, *Thirty Years War*, 420–21.

53. Wilson, *Thirty Years War*, 423.

54. Wilson, *Thirty Years War*, 448–49.

55. Wilson, *Thirty Years War*, 455–56.

56. J. H. Elliott, *Richelieu and Olivares* (Cambridge: Cambridge University Press, 1984), 119–21. Richelieu and the monarchy he served were plagued by the rebellion of Protestant Huguenots from 1621 to 1629, which crown forces brutally suppressed despite limited English support for the rebellion.

57. Wilson, *Thirty Years War*, 464. The annual cost of sustaining a soldier was 150 reichsthalers; thus, the French subsidy could sustain 2,666 soldiers, roughly 10 percent of Swedish strength.

58. For evidence of this, see the impact of Wallenstein's maneuvers on the shores of the Baltic Sea in the manifesto issued by Gustavus Adolphus upon his invasion of Germany, July 1630, in Helfferich, *Thirty Years War*, 101–2.

59. Wilson, *Thirty Years War*, 431; Michael Roberts, *Gustavus Adolphus*, 70–71.

60. "Gustavus said that if it [religion] had been the cause then he would have declared war on the pope." Wilson, *Thirty Years War*, 462.

61. Dodge, *Gustavus Adolphus*, 157.

62. Wilson, *Thirty Years War*, 459.

63. Parker, *Thirty Years' War*, 123.

64. Wilson, *Thirty Years War*, 467.

65. Wilson, *Thirty Years War*, 469–70.

66. "The Sack of Madgeburg (May 20, 1631)," in Helfferich, *Thirty Years War*, 109.

67. Cited in Peter H. Wilson, *The Thirty Years War: A Sourcebook* (New York: Palgrave MacMillan, 2010), 146.

68. C. R. L. Fletcher, *Gustavus Adolphus and the Struggle of Protestantism for Existence* (London: G. P. Putnam's Sons, 1890), 168.

69. Parker, *Thirty Years' War*, 125. Magdeburg came to symbolize the brutality of the Thirty Years' War. It took two centuries for the city's population to recover to its pre-siege level.

70. Dupuy, *Military Life*, 91.

71. At Werben Tilly's forces suffered 6,000 killed and injured while attempting to assault the Swedish army in its fortified positions. Dupuy, *Military Life*, 93.

72. Wilson, *Thirty Years War*, 470–72.

73. Parker, *Thirty Years' War*, 126.

74. Parker, *Thirty Years' War*, 126.

114Chapter 4

75. Wilson, *Thirty Years War*, 473–75; Parker, *Thirty Years' War*, 126; Dupuy, *Military Life*, 99–104; Dodge, *Gustavus Adolphus*, 258–69.

76. Parker, *Thirty Years' War*, 126.

77. Roberts, *Swedish Imperial Experience*, 52. Despite the vast expenses incurred by Swedish forces on the continent, only 4 percent of the state budget was spent on the war in Germany. Roberts, *Swedish Imperial Experience*, 53.

78. Wilson, *Thirty Years War*, 482.

79. The Swedish articles of war prescribed the death penalty for unauthorized plundering. Watts, "Swedish Discipline," 132.

80. Wilson, *Thirty Years War*, 483.

81. Roberts, *Gustavus Adolphus*, 126.

82. Roberts, *Swedish Imperial Experience*, 54.

83. Parker, *Thirty Years' War*, 172. After three decades of war, the Swedish adult male population declined precipitously. For example, the village of Bydeå in northern Sweden sent 230 men to serve in Poland and Germany in the 1620s and 1630s; only fifteen survived, and of these five were crippled. Parker, *Thirty Years' War*, 193.

84. Roberts, *Swedish Imperial Experience*, 44.

85. Wilson, *Thirty Years War*, 484.

86. Wilson, *Thirty Years War*, 492.

87. Tilly died on April 30, 1632, of wounds sustained at the Battle of the Lech.

88. Wilson, *Thirty Years War*, 493–94; strength number from 501.

89. Fletcher, *Gustavus Adolphus*, 262.

90. Wilson, *Thirty Years War*, 506.

91. Roberts, *History of Sweden*, 766.

92. Roberts, *History of Sweden*, 772. The battlefield of Lützen is still agricultural land, which has made it accessible to archaeologists who have endeavored to discover its secrets. For an overview of their work, see http://www.archaeologiestiftung.de/projekte/luetzen.

93. Roberts, *History of Sweden*, 773.

94. Dodge, *Gustavus Adolphus*, 52–53.

95. Parker, *Military Revolution*, 24.

96. Parker, *Military Revolution*, 133.

97. Parker, *Military Revolution*, 135.

98. Parker, *Military Revolution*, 137–38.

99. Parker, *Military Revolution*, 141. The Swedes lost twelve thousand men killed and four thousand captured, including the capable General Gustav Horn.

100. Quoted in Parker, *Military Revolution*, 156–57.

101. Wilson, *Thirty Years War*, 567–69.

102. Parker, *Thirty Years' War*, 177.

103. Geoffrey Parker, *Global Crisis: War, Climate Change & Catastrophe in the Seventeenth Century* (New Haven, CT: Yale University Press, 2013), 25.

104. Parker, *Thirty Years' War*, 183–86.

105. Roberts, *Gustavus Adolphus*, 192–93.

5

NAPOLEON'S ITALIAN CAMPAIGN

Andrew Roberts

Napoleon Bonaparte's reputation for military genius was founded upon the brilliant campaign the French army fought under his command in northern Italy against Austria from March 1796 to March 1797, in which he won a series of remarkable victories over armies often twice or thrice the size, commanded by generals far more experienced in warfare than the twenty-seven-year-old Corsican. In that twelve-month campaign he exhibited all the capacity for strategy, tactics, diplomacy, charisma, leadership, and flair that were to be seen in varying degrees later in his career. By routing the Austrians in northern Italy, a region they had controlled for eight decades, and doing so quickly, Napoleon set a standard for successful military campaigning that has rightly been studied by strategists ever since.

The French Revolution, which broke out in July 1789, was not yet seven years old when Napoleon embarked on the Italian campaign.[1] France had declared war against Austria in April 1792 and then Prussia and Piedmont in July, precipitating the War of the First Coalition. The Prussians and Austrians had invaded France in August, but were repulsed at the Battle of Valmy the following month. In November, the French government offered its assistance to all peoples wishing to overthrow their rulers. This was the world's first ideological war, in contrast to the traditional territorial and dynastic ones, and a decree was passed by the French Convention in December compelling all lands conquered by the

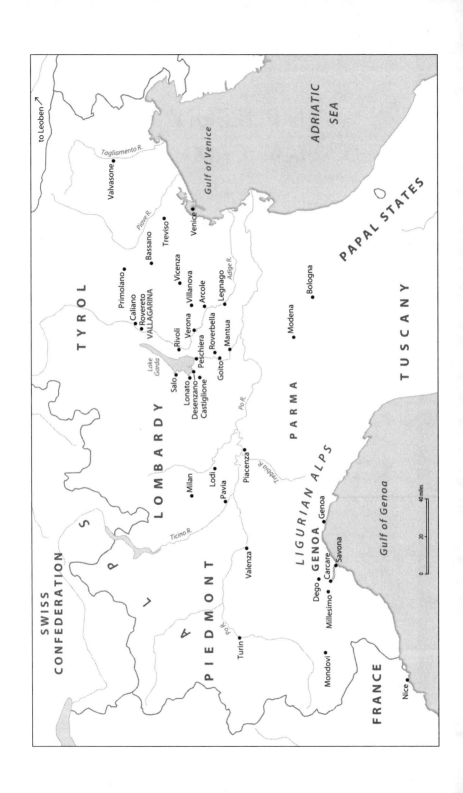

SWISS
CONFEDERATION

to Leoben ↗

Tagliamento R.

Valvasone

Piave R.

TYROL

Primolano

Caliano
Rovereto
VALLAGARINA

Bassano

Treviso

Venice

Gulf of Venice

ADRIATIC
SEA

PAPAL STATES

Vicenza
Villanova
Arcole
Legnago

Adige R.

Bologna

Rivoli
Verona
Peschiera
Roverbella
Mantua
Goito

*Lake
Garda*

Salo
Lonato
Desenzano
Castiglione

Modena

TUSCANY

P A R M A

Po R.

LOMBARDY

Milan
Lodi
Pavia

Piacenza

Trebbia R.

Ticino R.

LIGURIAN ALPS

Genoa
GENOA
Savona

Gulf of Genoa

Valenza

PIEDMONT

Dego
Carcare
Millesimo

Po R.

Turin

Mondovi

FRANCE

Nice

40 miles
0   20

A L P S

republican and atheist French Army to adopt their revolutionary laws and institutions.

After its execution of King Louis XVI in Paris in January 1793, the French government declared war on Britain and Holland in February, and Spain in March. With its population the largest in Europe (excluding Russia) at twenty-five million, in August it carried out a levy of all French males capable of serving. Thereafter, France invaded Holland in September, put down a Royalist uprising with remarkable ferocity in southwest France in October, and attempted to recapture the vital port of Toulon, which had been occupied by Coalition forces under Admiral Lord Hood since August. The general in charge of the all-important French artillery in the Toulon operation was the twenty-four-year-old Napoleon Bonaparte, who was made a general when, largely thanks to him, the city was recaptured in mid-December.

The years 1794 and 1795 saw immense internal political turmoil in France, with successive revolutionary factions executed by guillotine during the Reign of Terror, rampant inflation, and some military defeats, though also enough minor victories for France to survive, not least because of its large armies thanks to the levy. By March 1796 the Revolution was desperate for a decisive victory, and the Directory government chose to send Napoleon to Nice to undertake a campaign in the Po valley against the Austrians. The objectives of the campaign were fourfold: to protect France's southeastern flank; to strike a blow against Austria; to plunder northern Italy to help France's desperate financial plight; and to extend French revolutionary institutions to another part of Europe. Napoleon himself had a fifth, private, objective: to distinguish himself as a great commander, the equal of any of those of antiquity whose biographies he had voraciously read since childhood. Yet Italy was by no means the Directory's main focus of concentration, which was always closer to home on the Rhine and in Holland. Until Napoleon began to win his startling series of victories, the Italian campaign was considered only a sideshow for the government in Paris.

Napoleon was chosen to command the expeditionary force known as the Army of Italy as much for his political trustworthiness—he had brutally put down the Royalist uprising in Paris the previous October—as for any military capacity that the Directory had spotted in him. It also helped that his wife of only a few days, Joséphine de Beauharnais, had been the mistress of the leader of the Directory and de facto prime minister, Paul Barras. So when Napoleon arrived to take up his command at his headquarters in Nice on March 26, 1796, all five of his divisional commanders were prepared to despise him because, as one contemporary put it, he had "won his reputation in a street riot and his command in a marriage bed."[2] In fact, however, in a brief stint on the General Staff in Paris, then known as the Topographical Bureau, Napoleon had written no fewer than three detailed reports on how a campaign in Italy could be fought.

The divisional commanders were Jean Sérurier, who had thirty-four years of service; Pierre Augereau, a coarse thirty-eight-year-old former mercenary nicknamed "the proud brigand"; André Masséna, also thirty-eight, a former smuggler who had served at Toulon; Amédée Laharpe, a thirty-two-year-old Swiss; and Jean-Baptiste Meynier, whom Napoleon thought "incapable, not fit to command a battalion in a war as active as this one," but could not yet sack for political reasons.[3] All five were experienced veterans, whereas Napoleon had not so far commanded so much as an infantry battalion.

Napoleon threw himself into his new command with tremendous energy. He questioned the five generals on their divisions' position, equipment, morale, training, and numbers, all the while radiating perfect confidence in victory. He showed them how the Savona–Carcare road led to three valleys that could ultimately lead them into the rich plains of Lombardy if they could drive a wedge between the Austrian and Piedmontese armies and then force the latter to make peace by threatening their capital, Turin. It meant pitting forty-nine thousand three hundred French troops against eighty thousand of the enemy, but he would use speed and deception to retain the initiative and keep the enemy off balance.

During his excellent education at three military academies, Napoleon had read the works of military thinkers and reformers, and was now at last able to translate their ideas into action. Pierre de Bourcet's *Principes de la Guerre des Montagnes* (1775) and a strategy that had been aborted by Louis XV in 1745 proved helpful to Napoleon for his initial planning. In the campaign he would rely on a relentless concentration of effort, while keeping his opponents separated. He had ingested military textbooks constantly between the ages of nine and twenty-four, and now was about to fight a campaign that would appear in future ones.

The Army of Italy was utterly demoralized when Napoleon arrived. The men were freezing in threadbare uniforms without overcoats; no meat had been issued for three months; mules had pulled the artillery since the draft horses had died of malnutrition; entire battalions were shoeless or in clogs; many muskets lacked bayonets. Mutiny was in the air, as there had been no pay for months, and fever had killed six hundred men in one regiment in only twenty days. An eyewitness summed up their "wretched state" as "a total want of necessities, and a pestilential fever, the natural consequence of famine . . . dejected and enfeebled by sickness and destitute of horses, cannon, and almost every other sinew of war."[4] The results were potentially disastrous even before the campaign had begun. "Without bread the soldier tends to an excess of violence," Napoleon later wrote, "that makes one blush for being a man."[5] Yet Napoleon had only been given 40,000 francs by the Directory—less than his own annual salary—to pay for the entire campaign.

His response was to completely reorganize the commissariat and, as he reported to the Directory, "threaten the contractors, who have robbed much and who enjoy credit."[6] He also took out a 3 million franc line of credit from a consortium of Genoan financiers, on his own authority and without the Directory's collateral. Within two days of arriving in Nice, Napoleon had also disbanded the mutinous Third Battalion of the 209th Demi-Brigade and court-martialed two officers for crying *"Vive le roi!"* His energy and capacity for hard work quickly impressed his divisional commanders: he wrote more than eight hundred dispatches over the next nine months, micromanaging every conceivable subject, such as where drummer-boys should stand on parade and the conditions under which "La Marseillaise" could be played. He was particularly concerned about the lack of footwear in the Army of Italy, and used his political connections in Paris to get five thousand pairs of shoes delivered before the campaign started. Legend has Napoleon saying, possibly apocryphally, "An army marches on its stomach," but he was certainly highly conscious that it marched on its feet. He also took to making inspirational proclamations and Orders of the Day. These were issued by the forty-three-year-old Louis-Alexandre Berthier, a former engineer who had fought in the American War of Independence; he became Napoleon's chief of staff, a position he was to retain until 1814. Napoleon was the first commander to employ a chief of staff in its modern sense, and Berthier was superb at his job, capable of expressing Napoleon's wishes accurately and succinctly. He had a capacious memory but his efficient staff also devised an advanced filing system to record where every unit of the Army was at any particular time.

Napoleon hoped to outmaneuver the cautious, seventy-one-year-old Austrian commander, Johann Beaulieu, in the mountains around Montenotte in the Ligurian Alps. He adopted "the strategy of the central position" whereby he would place himself at the hinge between the two enemy forces and strike first at one and then at the other before they could coalesce. It was a strategy to which he would adhere throughout his career, with extraordinary success. He had planned to launch his offensive on April 15, but Beaulieu unexpectedly started his own five days earlier, coming up the same road that Napoleon had intended to go down. Within two days, Napoleon had rescued the situation and organized a counterattack. On the evening of April 11, realizing that the Austrian line was overextended, he fixed the enemy in place with an attack at Montenotte, and then sent Masséna around the right flank in the pouring rain at 1 a.m. to envelop them. There were a series of mountain peaks between two thousand and three thousand feet high, with thick vegetation, but they were success-fully crossed by the swift-moving French infantry columns.

Despite being a relatively modest engagement, Montenotte was Napoleon's first victory in the field as a commander in chief. Several of his future battles were to follow the same parameters: an elderly opponent lacking energy; a nationally and linguisti-cally diverse enemy confronting the homogenous French army; a vulnerable spot that Napoleon would latch on to and not let go; and a well-timed flanking maneuver under a talented sub-ordinate. The French had moved significantly faster than their enemy, and Napoleon had employed a concentration of forces that reversed the numerical odds for just long enough to prove decisive in his favor.

Napoleon never wasted time after a victory during this cam-paign. The day after Montenotte, he fought another engagement at Millesimo, where he kept the retreating Austrian and Pied-montese forces apart. At the fortified village of Dego, Napoleon won his third victory in three days. Austro-Piedmontese losses numbered around 5,700 while the French lost 1,500. These were not large engagements, but they were strategically vital in sepa-rating the Austrians and Piedmontese. A week later at Mondovi, he attempted a double-envelopment against the latter. It was an ambitious and difficult maneuver to pull off but devastating to enemy morale when it succeeded. The following day the Pied-montese sued for peace.

"Today you equal by your services the armies of Holland and the Rhine," Napoleon told his men on April 26. "Devoid of everything, you supplied everything. You have won battles with-out guns; passed rivers without bridges; accomplished forced marches without shoes; bivouacked without brandy and often without bread. . . . Today you are amply provided for."[7] A victori-ous, hungry army tends to pillage. Napoleon did not like the fact, and threatened to shoot troops caught doing so, but he never did. He differentiated between "living off the land" (light pillaging), which his army had to do because the Directory had left them unsupplied, and what he himself called "fearful pillage."[8] Living off the land permitted his armies the speed to maneuver that was essential to his strategy. "The strength of the army," he stated, "like power in mechanics, is the product of multiplying the mass by the velocity."[9] A normal distance covered of fifteen miles a day could be doubled under forced marches. In the warm spring Italian weather, Napoleon's men did not need tents, and, as one veteran recalled, they "marched so rapidly that they could not have carried with them all the requisite baggage."[10] Lighter field guns, more and better roads, and smaller baggage trains than earlier in the century meant that Napoleon's armies could move at what he himself calculated to be twice the speed of Julius Caesar's.

The Piedmontese signed the peace treaty on April 28. In a secret clause, Napoleon secured the right to use their bridge over the river Po at Valenza, knowing that this information would be quickly leaked to the Austrians and Beaulieu would therefore send troops there. Yet he had already planned to cross the river near Piacenza, seventy miles to the west. "My columns are on the march," he told the Directory. "Beaulieu is flying, but I hope to overtake him."[11] He also started levying what he euphemistically termed "contributions" of several million francs on the rulers of the territories he was conquering, which allowed him both to send specie to Paris and to start paying his men in silver rather than the despised assignat paper money, which was almost worthless. He also intended to do his own pillaging, of works of art that he could take to Paris and display in the Louvre. "Send me a list," he asked one of his confederates, "of the pictures, statues, *cabinets* and curiosities at Milan, Parma, Piacenza, Modena and Bologna."[12]

Beaulieu had meanwhile retreated into the angle of the Po and Ticino Rivers, covering Pavia and Milan, with his lines of communication running north of the Po. Napoleon made a dash for Piacenza, bypassing several river defense lines and threatening Milan. This was the first example of what was to become another favored strategy, the *manoeuvre sur les derrières*, getting behind his enemy. Beaulieu was a day's march closer to Piacenza, so Napoleon asked his men to march even faster, confident that he and

Berthier had calculated every supply requirement (especially the ammunition) in detail. While Sérurier and Masséna moved to Valenza to deceive Beaulieu, and Augereau added to the confusion by taking up a post midway between Valenza and Piacenza, cutting all cross-river communications, Napoleon rushed forward through the neutral Dukedom of Parma, not allowing any niceties of international law to detain him.

By dawn on May 7, the French army was ready to cross the Po where it joined the Trebbia. Napoleon himself crossed on May 8 and headed straight to Piacenza, whose governor opened the city gates for him after it was made clear to him what would happen to his city otherwise. "One more victory," Napoleon predicted to the Directory, "and we are masters of Italy." By May 10, the Austrian army was retreating toward Milan via the town of Lodi, twenty-two miles southeast of Milan on the right bank of the river Adda. Hoping to intercept them, Napoleon sent his trusted lieutenants, Generals Auguste Marmont and Jean Lannes, to chase the Austrian rear guard through the town until they were halted by canister shot from the other end of a two-hundred-yard-long and ten-yard-wide wooden bridge. Using his talents as an artilleryman, Napoleon personally commandeered two cannon and prevented the enemy from destroying the bridge. Personal intervention when the occasion demanded was another aspect of his hands-on leadership technique. "A general's most important talent is to know the mind of the soldier and gain his confidence," Napoleon was later to tell one of his ministers, "and in both respects the French soldier is more difficult to lead than another. He's not a machine that must be made to move, he's a reasonable being who needs leadership."[13]

Napoleon decided that the bridge would have to be stormed immediately. The first soldiers sent onto it after a harangue (inspirational speech) from him were cut down and flung back, but he sent in further waves of men, under the command of Berthier, Lannes, and then Masséna. With great bravery, the bridge was taken and held, despite fierce Austrian counterattacks. "On 15 May 1796," wrote Henri Stendhal in his novel *The Charterhouse of*

Parma, "General Bonaparte made his entry into Milan at the head of a youthful army which had just crossed the bridge at Lodi and let the world know that after all these centuries, Caesar and Alexander had a successor."

The storming of the bridge at Lodi quickly became a central part of the Napoleonic legend, even though Napoleon had only faced the Austrian rear guard and each side had lost equal numbers of men in the engagement. After the battle, Napoleon acquired the nickname *le Petit Caporal* (the little corporal), an example of victorious soldiers affectionately teasing commanders they admire. The mutinous talk had meanwhile been replaced by a powerful sense of esprit de corps. "I no longer regarded myself as a simple general," Napoleon later said of his victory at Lodi, "but as a man called upon to decide the fate of peoples. It came to me then that I really could become a decisive actor on our national stage."[14]

He told the Directory that if he could take the near-impregnable city of Mantua, where Beaulieu was heading, he believed he could be in the heart of Austria itself within three weeks. He also reported that he had lost one hundred fifty men against Austria's two to three thousand, which was quite untrue as the real numbers—as he well knew—were closer to nine hundred casualties on each side. Napoleon's regular exaggeration of enemy losses and diminution of his own came to be a persistent feature of his self-mythologizing. Writing to Joséphine after one battle, he put down the number of his wounded as seven hundred before scribbling it out and inserting one hundred instead.[15] Propaganda and myth-making were second nature to him, knowing that fake news was excellent for morale—at least until, years later, it led to the French expression that translates as "to lie like a bulletin."

Once he had established himself at the magnificent Palazzo Serbelloni in Milan, Napoleon began to entertain on a lavish scale, giving audiences to local Italian authors, newspaper editors, aristocrats, scientists, intellectuals, sculptors, and opera singers, presenting himself as an enlightened liberator. He promoted the idea of an independent Italian nation-state that would be embraced by progressive Italians. He meanwhile set about abolishing the old Austrian governing institutions, reforming Pavia University, holding provisional municipal elections, founding a National Guard, and devolving power to Italians wherever he could. Of course, he also imposed a massive 20 million franc "contribution" from Lombardy. He reformed northern Italy with the collaboration of pro-French Italian middle-class revolutionaries, even while he was mulcting it financially for the benefit of France and his troops. Napoleon used politics in the Italian campaign as an invaluable adjunct to what he was trying to do militarily, which was to expel the Austrians from Italy.

Reforms that Napoleon imposed on the newly conquered territories included the abolition of internal tariffs, assemblies of noblemen, and feudal privileges; measures of tax reform; the end of the guild system that restrained trade and industry; and the imposition of religious toleration as he closed the Jewish ghettos and allowed Jews to live outside them for the first time in centuries. These modernizing initiatives, which were repeated in most of the territories he conquered over the coming decade, brought genuinely enlightened government to some parts of Europe, though because of the crushing expense of almost perpetual war they could rarely flourish as Napoleon had intended.

On May 23 a revolt against the French occupation led by Catholic priests in Pavia was put down harshly on Napoleon's orders. "Nothing is more salutary than terrible examples aptly given," he wrote of this incident at the time.[16] "If you make war," he added three years later, "wage it with energy and severity; it is the only means of making it shorter and consequently less deplorable for Mankind." He could use both carrot and stick with recalcitrant populations. "The French army love and respect all people, more especially the simple and virtuous inhabitants of the mountains," read one of his proclamations to the Tyrolese that month. "But should you ignore your own interests, and take up arms, we shall be terrible as the fire from heaven."[17] After further defeats in late May, Beaulieu was replaced as overall Austrian commander by Marshal General Dagobert von Wurmser, another septuagenarian.

Four fortresses—Mantua, Peschiera, Legnago, and Verona— held the key to Austrian power in northern Italy. Known as the Quadrilateral, together they protected the entrance to the Alpine passes to the north and east as well as the approaches to the Po and Lake Garda. On June 2, 1796, Napoleon began his siege of the well-provisioned Mantua, which is surrounded on three sides by water. His forces were stretched to the breaking point, as he had not yet captured the Citadel of Milan, had to guard against Austrian relief forces arriving from the Tyrol, and had to quell the Pavian uprising before it spread further. He was also under orders from the Directory to extend the Revolution southward into the Papal States and expel the Royal Navy from Livorno. Napoleon generally liked to keep his movements fluid and to avoid sieges, and he had only 40,400 men with which to besiege Mantua, keep communication routes open, and hold the line of the river Adige.

Mantua, commanded by Beaulieu, was under siege for all but five weeks of the next eight months between June 1796 and February 1797. As it began, Napoleon entered Modena on June 18 and Bologna the next day, where he expelled the papal authorities and forced Pope Pius VI to sign an armistice and make a "contribution" of 15 million francs. But Wurmser was now on his way south with fifty thousand men, and by late July Napoleon had learned that he would be taking his army down both sides of Lake Garda to relieve Mantua, where sickness was starting to wear down Beaulieu's garrison. Napoleon relied a good deal on intelligence in his campaigns, which he insisted on analyzing personally rather than having it sifted through by staff officers, so he could decide for himself how much credence to attach to each piece.

Wurmser himself went down the eastern side of Lake Garda with 32,000 men in five columns, while the Croatian-born cavalryman General Peter von Quasdanovich went down the western side with 18,000 men. Napoleon installed Sérurier with 10,500 men to maintain the siege of Mantua, leaving him with 31,300 men to meet the new threats. He sent 4,400 to Salo to slow down Quasdanovich, ordered Masséna to the eastern side with 15,400 men, deployed 4,700 to protect the Peschiera–Verona line, sent Augereau with 5,300 to watch the roads from the east, and kept 1,500 cavalry in reserve. He then moved continually between Brescia, Castelnuovo, Desenzano, Roverbello, Castiglione, Goïto, and Peschiera, going to wherever he was needed the most. The severe summer heat led to his riding five horses to death in quick succession at that time.

Napoleon was so short of men that on July 30 he even ordered Sérurier to end the siege of Mantua and march to join him. This involved abandoning no fewer than 179 cannon and mortars, and dumping their ammunition in the lakes. It pained him, but he knew that the decisive victories of modern warfare were to be found in the field, not in fortresses. In a series of battles around Lonato in early August and at Castiglione on August 15, Napoleon defeated Wurmser's attempt to relieve Mantua, and was aided by the fact that Beaulieu's emaciated forces were too physically weak to sally out of the city behind him.

The battles at Lonato and Castiglione saw Napoleon use the *bataillon carré* system. Although invented by the authors Jacques de Guibert and Pierre de Bourcet in textbook form in the 1760s and 1770s, it was Napoleon who first put it into practice successfully on the battlefield. Under its diamond-shaped formation of units, if the main body of the enemy was encountered, say, on the right flank, the division on the right became the new advance guard whose job it was to fix the enemy in place. The divisions that had formed the old vanguard and rear guard then automatically became the *masse de manoeuvre*, the central strike force capable of supporting the new advance division, with the aim of enveloping the enemy's flanks. The army could therefore turn ninety degrees in either direction with relative ease. What Bourcet had called "controlled dispersion" allowed Napoleon the extra flexibility necessary to adapt his battlefront constantly, which proved invaluable in the fast-moving, almost constant battles of this period of the campaign.

Having repulsed Wurmser, Napoleon resumed the siege of Mantua on August 10. It still held 16,400 Austrian soldiers within its ten-foot-thick walls, although less than three-quarters of them were fit for duty. In late August he learned that Wurmser was about to make a second attempt to relieve Mantua. Combing out his lines of communication and receiving some men from the Army of the Alps gave Napoleon a total of over 50,000 troops. By September 2 he knew for certain that Wurmser was coming down the Lagarina valley of the Adige. He advanced to Rovereto, where he intercepted the Austrian advance guard on September 4 and sent it into full retreat. Four more battles were fought up the valley over the following week. At Calliano the French surprised the Austrians at breakfast, and forced them out of their positions. At Primolano on September 7, the French attacked a seemingly impregnable position and carried it by sheer élan. That night Napoleon slept with Augereau's division, wrapped in his cloak and sharing their rations. The next day they captured two thousand Austrians and thirty guns at Bassano, along with several ammunition wagons. The sheer tempo of the operations ensured that he had always kept the initiative, bowling unstoppably along a narrow valley gorge replete with places where the Austrians should have been able to slow down or halt him, but could not. This lightning campaign up the Adige was the perfect illustration of why high esprit de corps was so valuable, keeping up the pressure on Wurmser with regular dawn attacks.

By October 10, Wurmser and his 14,000 men had joined the 16,000 already bottled up in Mantua. With 4,000 men dying of wounds, malnutrition, and disease in six weeks, and a further 7,000 in hospital, and with only thirty-eight days of food left, the city could not hold out very much longer. "The brave should be facing danger, not swamp plague," Napoleon wrote to Wurmser, urging his surrender, to no avail. In early November, the Hungarian veteran General József Alvinczi arrived to lead a third Austrian attempt to relieve the city, hoping his 28,000 men would drive the French back from Rivoli to Mantua, while General Giovanni di Provera advanced with 9,000 men from Brenta to Legnago as a diversion, and 10,000 men at Bassano tried to prevent Napoleon from concentrating his forces. Napoleon later said that the sixty-one-year-old Alvinczi was the best general he had fought thus far, which was why he never said anything either positive or negative about him in his bulletins. (By contrast he praised Beaulieu, Wurmser, and Provera, whom he did not rate and did not want replaced.)

Napoleon positioned his forces as far south as possible to give him maximum warning of where and when the Austrians were coming. Alvinczi crossed the Piave River on November 2, ordering Quasdanovich to march on Vicenza via Bassano, and Provera to go there via Treviso. It was always an error to split one's forces in front of Napoleon, who devised a very bold plan to get behind Alvinczi at Villanova and force him to fight for his line of retreat in country so flooded with rice fields that his much larger numbers would count for little. The key town of Arcole was strongly held—loopholed and barricaded—by the Austrians, and Napoleon arrived at the bridge there just as Augereau's first attempt to capture it had been beaten off. Surrounded by his aides-de-camp and bodyguard, Napoleon grasped a tricolor and led a charge himself, haranguing the troops about their heroism at Lodi. His aide-de-camp, Colonel Muiron, and others were killed on the bridge at Napoleon's side, and Napoleon himself had to be bundled off the causeway into the marshy ground behind the bridge. He had nonetheless once again shown his personal bravery under fire.

As winter closed in and the fighting season ended with Mantua still under siege, the Austrians made their fourth attempt at its relief. The campaign had cost Austria nearly 18,000 casualties, and the French more than 19,000. The French were now short of everything—officers, shoes, medicine, and pay. On January 7, 1797, Napoleon discovered that the Austrians were again moving south, this time with 47,000 troops. Once again they split their forces down each side of Lake Garda. Napoleon immediately left Milan and made multiple visits to Bologna, Verona, and his headquarters at Roverbello. He had 37,000 men in the field and 8,500 under Sérurier in the Mantuan siege lines.

Divining through his almost instinctive sense of psychology and understanding of topography which Austrian advance was the feint (Provera's) and which the genuine threat (Quasdano-vich's), on the night of January 13 Napoleon fired off orders completely reorganizing his army just prior to a major battle at Rivoli, along the lines of the old military maxim, "March separately, fight together." He recognized the next day that the plateau above the gorges there would be the key deciding place—in military terms the *point d'appui*, or *Schwerpunkt*—of the battle, knowing the area intimately, having ridden across it often over the previous four months. Rivoli was a hard-fought contest—the Austrians were a brave and tenacious enemy—but by 2 p.m. they were in full retreat. Napoleon's pursuit had only to be abandoned when news came from Augereau that Provera had crossed the Adige and was heading for Mantua, whereupon Masséna was sent off to help Augereau prevent its relief. This was effected just in time at the village of La Favorita, outside Mantua itself.

On February 2, 1797, Wurmser was forced to surrender Mantua and its emaciated garrison. Some 16,300 Austrians had died there over the course of the previous eight months, and many more civilians, who had been reduced to eating rats and dogs. Not only did the French capture 325 Austrian guns, but they also retook the 179 they had been forced to abandon back in August. Napoleon wasn't present to witness his triumph. He had gone to Verona and then Bologna to punish the Papal States for threatening to rise in Austria's support despite the armistice they had signed the previous June. By February 17 the Pope was suing for peace again, and promised to pay a "contribution" of 30 million francs and one hundred works of art. "We will have everything that is beautiful in Italy," Napoleon told the Directory, "with the exception of a small number of objects at Turin and Naples."[18]

On March 10, he set off on a northern campaign to force the Austrians to call an armistice. It was risky taking a force of only 40,000 men through the Tyrol to Klagenfurt and eventually to Leoben in Styria, not far from Vienna itself. On March 16 he crossed the Tagliamento River and inflicted a small defeat on the Emperor of Austria's brother, the Archduke Charles Hapsburg, at Valvasone. It was there that Napoleon introduced the *ordre mixte*—a compromise between attacking in line and attacking in column first developed by Guibert to cope with the vagaries of a terrain that did not permit regular deployments. Napoleon employed it again a few days later while crossing the Isonzo into Austria, on both occasions intervening personally to create a formation that combined the firepower of a battalion in line with the attack weight of two battalions in column.

Fearful of losing their capital to Napoleon's drive and thrust, on April 2 the Austrians accepted Napoleon's offer of an armistice at Leoben, a little over one hundred miles southwest of Vienna.

In one year of campaigning, Napoleon had crossed the Apennines and the Alps, defeated the Piedmontese and no fewer than six Austrian armies, and inflicted 120,000 casualties. He had wrung peace treaties from the Pope and the kings of Piedmont and Naples as well as several northern Italian dukes, abolished the medieval dukedom of Modena, and defeated in every conceivable set of military circumstances most of Austria's most celebrated generals, including Beaulieu, Wurmser, Provera, Quasdanovich, and Alvinczi, who had almost always outnumbered him in total—though not on the battlefields, which he had chosen with an unerring eye, cleaving to the strategy of the central position. As well as making a close study of the history and geography of Italy, a place he had not visited before the campaign, Napoleon was ready to experiment with the ideas of others, most notably the concepts of the *bataillon carré* and the *ordre mixte*. He had chosen his commanders well, and sacked those who had not made the grade, including Meynier. Napoleon's prodigious memory, fascination with logistics, and great calmness under pressure also helped him to win twelve victories in as many months.

When analyzing those individual victories, it is remarkable how varied his tactics had been. At Montenotte he pinned the enemy to the front and turned the right flank. Millesimo was in pursuit of a retreating enemy. At Dego he had rescued a potential defeat by personally arriving and channeling everything available into the struggle. Mondovi had seen a vigorous frontal-fixing attack and an attempted double-envelopment. A massive frontal assault at Lodi was assisted by a flanking cavalry movement. At Lonato he had checked an enemy offensive to his rear and counterattacked centrally while turning the right flank. Castiglione had seen him trapping the enemy between two armies and taking them from the rear. At Rovereto and at Arcole he had turned the Austrians' left flank. Primolano and Bassano had been pursuits of a retreating enemy. Mantua had shown his persistence in siege-making, and finally Rivoli had been an exercise in counterattacking against an assault on his rear. The sheer versatility of the Italian campaign was a revelation in a commander who was still only twenty-seven when it ended.

The fact that the Army of Italy was in a position to fight at all, considering the privations from which it was suffering when Napoleon took over its command, was a testament to his energy and organizational abilities. His leadership qualities—acting with harshness when he thought it was deserved to units that had underperformed, but lavishing high praise on other occasions—produced the esprit de corps so necessary for victory. "In war," Napoleon was to say in 1808, "moral factors account for three-quarters of the whole; relative material strength accounts for only one-quarter."[19] His personal courage further bonded him to his men.

He was, needless to say, hugely helped by the way that the Austrians kept on sending septuagenarian commanders against him who continually split their forces and moved at around half the speed of the French. That was an advantage that would not continue as the Napoleonic Wars progressed, once the Coalition commanders learned from their predecessors' mistakes.

It was Napoleon's success in Italy that was to lead to his Egyptian command in 1798, and ultimately gave him the prestige that allowed him to pull off his coup d'état in Brumaire (November 1799), and it thus had profound geopolitical consequences far removed from the Italian peninsula itself. The military lessons to be derived from the Italian campaign are fairly universal and widespread, but rarely have they been laid out so comprehensively as in that twelve-month campaign. According to the excellent *Napoléon: Stratège* exhibition at the Musée de l'Armée at Les Invalides in Paris in the spring of 2018, his campaigns have been studied—at least as interpreted by military historians such as Henri Jomini, Carl von Clausewitz, Alfred Thayer Mahan, and Basil Liddell Hart—by military commanders as varied as (in no particular order) George S. Patton, Georgy Zhukov, Erwin Rommel, Erich von Manstein, Norman Schwarzkopf, Douglas MacArthur, Joseph Joffre, and Helmuth von Moltke, as well as George C. Marshall, Colin Powell, Robert E. Lee, Ulysses S. Grant, and many more.[20] Indeed, it would probably be easier to list those generals who have *not* in some way been influenced by this great captain of history than the ones who have (and they would make a far less distinguished list).

Even during the wars that were named after him, Coalition commanders such as the Duke of Wellington, Marshal Mikhail Kutuzov, and Prince Karl-Philipp Schwarzenberg made a close inspection of Napoleon's campaigning techniques in order to try to divine what he might do next. They were not always successful in this. He was, after all, Napoleon.

RECOMMENDATIONS FOR FURTHER READING

Despite its being published over half a century ago, David Chandler's monumental *The Campaigns of Napoleon* (New York: Macmillan, 1966) is still the best work to study for all the seven Wars of the Coalitions. More recent works that are also worth reading are Michael Broers's *Napoleon: Soldier of Destiny* (London: Faber and Faber, 2014) and the newly published *Napoleon: A Life* (New York: Basic Books, 2018) by Adam Zamoyski. Martin Boycott-Brown's *The Road to Rivoli: Napoleon's First Campaign* (London: Cassell, 2001) is useful too, and if one is looking for a fully revisionist account one can read Owen Connelly's controversial but well-researched *Blundering to Glory: Napoleon's Military Campaigns* (Wilmington, DE: Scholarly Resources, 1993). For the political, financial, and religious reforms that Napoleon effected, see

Michael Broers's *The Napoleonic Empire in Italy, 1796–1814: Cultural Imperialism in a European Context?* (New York: Palgrave Macmillan, 2005). Two older, but still serviceable, accounts are Herbert H. Sargent's *Napoleon Bonaparte's First Campaign* (Chicago: A. C. McClurg and Company, 1895) and Paul Gaffarel's *Bonaparte et les Républiques Italiennes (1796–1799)* (Paris: Félix Alcan, 1895). Jean Tranié and Juan-Carlos Carmigniani, *Napoléon Bonaparte: La Première Campagne D'Italie: 1796–1797* (Paris: Pygmalion G. Watelet, 1990) is also very good, and plenty of interesting insights can be found in Fletcher Pratt, "Vignettes of Napoleon in Italy 1796," *Journal of American Military History* 2, no. 2 (Summer 1938): 59–69. *Attack in the West: Napoleon's First Campaign Re-Read Today* (London: Eyre & Spottiswoode, 1953) by W. G. F. Jackson is a good old-fashioned overview, while Phillip R. Cuccia's *Napoleon in Italy: The Sieges of Mantua, 1796–1799* (Norman: University of Oklahoma Press, 2014) is a good modern account of one of the central features of the campaign. There are a large number of excellent and fascinating contemporary and near-contemporary accounts, two of which are François René Jean de Pommereul, *Campaign of General Bonaparte in Italy, 1796–7. By a general officer. Translated from the French, and continued to the Treaty of Campo Formio, by T. E. Ritchie* (2nd ed. London: T. E. Ritchie, 1800), and the reminiscences of an Englishwoman living in Florence at the time, published in Mariana Starke's *Letters from Italy between the Years 1792 and 1798*, 2 vols. (London: T. Gillet, 1800).

NOTES

1. Known to historians as the First Italian Campaign, to differentiate it from the very short Second Italian Campaign of 1800 that involved Napoleon taking the Grande Armée across the Alps, and which ended shortly after Napoleon's victory at the battle of Marengo in June.

2. Fletcher Pratt, "Vignettes of Napoleon in Italy 1796," *Journal of American Military History* 2, no. 2 (Summer 1938): 60.

3. Martin Boycott-Brown, *The Road to Rivoli* (London: Cassell, 2001), 412.

4. Mariana Starke, *Letters from Italy between the Years 1792 and 1798* (London: T. Gillet, 1800), 217–19.

5. Jay Luvaas, ed., *Napoleon on the Art of War* (New York: The Free Press, 1999), 10.

6. Fondation Napoléon, *Correspondance générale* I, no. 426 [March 28, 1796] (Paris: Fayard, 2004), 304.

7. D. A. Bingham, ed., *A Selection from the Letters and Dispatches of the First Napoleon*, vol. I (London: Chapman and Hall, Limited, 1884), 74 [April 26, 1796].

8. Bingham, *Letters and Dispatches*, 71–72 [April 22, 1796].

9. David G. Chandler, *The Military Maxims of Napoleon* (London: Greenhill Books, 1987), 111.

10. Elzéar Blaze, *Life in Napoleon's Army: The Memoirs of Captain Elzéar Blaze* (Barnsley, UK: Frontline Books, 1995), 145.

11. Fondation Napoléon, *Correspondance générale* I, no. 545 [April 20, 1796], 370.

12. Fondation Napoléon, *Correspondance générale* I, no. 557 [May 1, 1796], 377.

13. Jean-Antoine Chaptal, *Mes souvenirs sur Napoléon* (Paris: E. Plon, Nourrit et Cie., 1893), 296.

14. Jean Tulard, *Napoléon: Les grands moments d'un destin* (Paris: Fayard, 2006), 97.

15. Leon Cerf, ed., *Letters of Napoleon to Josephine* (1931), 37–40.

16. Bruno Colson, ed., *Napoleon on War* (Oxford: Oxford University Press, 2015), 342.

17. Bingham, *Letters and Dispatches*, 96 [June 14, 1796].

18. Fondation Napoléon, *Correspondance générale* I, no. 1395, 849 [February 19, 1797].

19. Colonel Bernd Horn and Robert W. Walker, eds., *Le précis de leadership militaire* (Toronto: Dundurn Press, 2008), 485.

20. Émile Robbe and François Lagrange, eds., *Napoléon: Stratège* (Paris: Lienart, 2018), 276–77.

6

THE SINO-AMERICAN LITTORAL WAR OF 2025: A FUTURE HISTORY

Michael R. Auslin

More than two decades after the fact, the reasons why the United States and the People's Republic of China (PRC) avoided total war, let alone a nuclear exchange, during their armed conflict in the autumn of 2025 remain a source of dispute. What is clearer is why the Sino-American Littoral War broke out in the first place and the course it took. The result—the establishment of three geopolitical blocs in East Asia—continues to this day. The United States retained a rump alliance system, but the losses of Taiwan and the US alliance with South Korea were seen as major strategic defeats for Washington, leading to a tacit US withdrawal from the western Pacific. On the other hand, though seemingly victorious in the war, China's subsequent domination over a resentful bloc of allies and its broader diplomatic isolation narrowed the range of foreign policy initiatives that Beijing's military superiority should have made possible. The resulting cold war between the United States and China became the defining feature of geopolitics in the Asia-Pacific in the middle of the twenty-first century.

To understand what happened and why, any history must start with the political environment between Washington and Beijing in the years leading up to the war, as well as look at the military

---

This essay also appeared in Michael R. Auslin, *Asia's New Geopolitics: Essays on Reshaping the Indo-Pacific* (Stanford, CA: Hoover Institution Press, 2020).

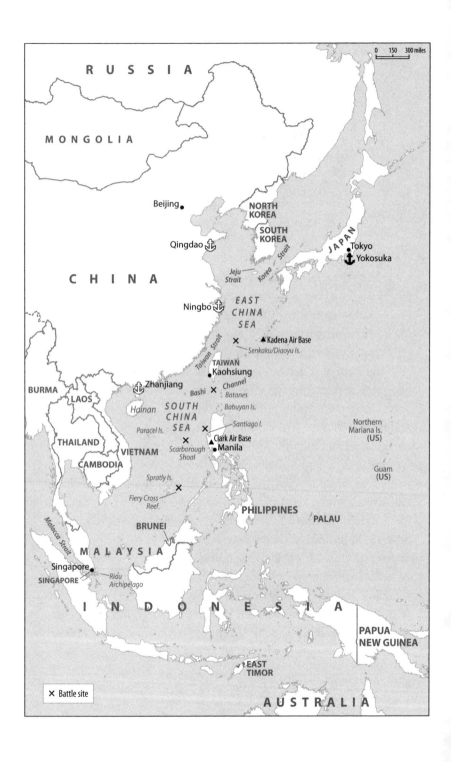

0   150   300 miles

R U S S I A

M O N G O L I A

Beijing•

NORTH
KOREA

SOUTH
KOREA

Qingdao⚓

Jeju
Strait

Korea Strait

J A P A N Tokyo•
⚓Yokosuka

C H I N A

Ningbo⚓

EAST
CHINA
SEA

✕ ▲Kadena Air Base
    Senkaku/Diaoyu Is.

TAIWAN
Kaohsiung•

Taiwan Strait

BURMA

LAOS

⚓Zhanjiang

Hainan

Bashi ✕ Channel
        Batanes
        Babuyan Is.

THAILAND

VIETNAM

CAMBODIA

SOUTH
CHINA
SEA

Paracel Is. ✕

✕
Scarborough
Shoal

Santiago I.

✕
▲Clark Air Base
•Manila

Northern
Mariana Is.
(US)

Guam
(US)

Spratly Is.

✕
Fiery Cross
Reef

PHILIPPINES   PALAU

Malacca Strait

BRUNEI

M A L A Y S I A

Singapore•
SINGAPORE Riau
            Archipelago

I N D O N E S I A

PAPUA
NEW GUINEA

✕ Battle site

EAST
TIMOR

A U S T R A L I A

assets each possessed and assess the balance of power in the western Pacific at the outset of hostilities. Only then will analysts be able to interpret the political and military decisions taken by both sides.

THE POLITICAL BACKGROUND

The influence of existing political relations on subsequent policy decisions is often downplayed by historians attempting to assert that rational actors had clearly articulated reasons for choosing a path that led to armed conflict. Yet the decade before the outbreak of war between China and America witnessed a steady erosion in Sino-US relations that poisoned the various links built up between the two nations since the 1970s and made crisis management increasingly difficult. The Cold War paradigm established by Richard Nixon and Jimmy Carter, where the United States sought to play the PRC and Soviet Union off each other, had evolved during the Reagan administration into a more transactional approach that sought to develop Sino-US relations for their own sake while attempting to get Beijing's support for US policies that pressured Moscow, such as in Afghanistan and Cambodia.

With the end of the Cold War, American policy makers turned to constructing a new great-power relationship with China, despite growing strains between the two countries. Though the George H. W. Bush administration largely downplayed the regime's Tiananmen Square massacre of prodemocracy student demonstrators in June 1989, the Clinton administration sent two aircraft carriers to the Taiwan Strait in March 1996 after Beijing fired ballistic missiles off the island during Taiwan's first presidential campaign.[1] Yet under administrations of both political parties, Washington steadily attempted to integrate China into what liberal internationalists called the "rules-based international order." Thus, the Clinton and George W. Bush administrations midwifed the PRC's entrance into the World Trade Organization, and successive US leaders ignored growing evidence of China's industrial and cyber espionage of both US government and private American business secrets. The 1999 Cox Commission Report detailed how Chinese agents stole some of America's most sensitive nuclear and ballistic missile technology, and a later report by Mandiant Corporation, in February 2013, revealed years of cyber espionage against a variety of US targets.[2]

However, it was during the Barack Obama administration that the real seeds of the 2025 Littoral War were laid. Building off the Bush administration's elevation of high-level bilateral talks into the "Strategic and Economic Dialogue," the Obama administration energetically engaged the Chinese government. Ostensibly pushing back against Beijing's rampant cyber espionage, Obama and new Chinese leader Xi Jinping agreed at the 2013 Sunnylands Summit that China would rein in its official and quasi-official hackers.[3] Like his predecessors, Obama traveled to China, though his 2016 visit revealed strains in bilateral ties when he was subjected to protocol insults on his arrival at the airport and hotel.[4]

Petty jockeying aside, however, serious challenges to Asian regional stability emerged during Obama's two terms. Most egregious was Beijing's decision to build and fortify islands in disputed maritime territory in the South China Sea. Ownership of various coral reefs and shoals in the Spratly and Paracel island chains had long been contested between China and a host of Southeast Asian countries. Many had built modest defensive installations on some of their possessions, yet Beijing claimed that then secretary of state Hillary Clinton's comments at a regional security meeting in 2010 demonstrated US antagonism toward China's rightful claims.[5] Clinton had stated that the Obama administration considered the peaceful multilateral resolution of competing territorial claims to be in the United States' national interest. Clinton's statements were combined with articulation of a "rebalance" or "pivot" to Asia, an assertion by Obama officials that the Asia-Pacific was the key geopolitical focus for America. To buttress the pivot, in addition to a new multilateral free-trade agreement, the Trans-Pacific Partnership (TPP), the Pentagon announced increased troop deployments to the Asia-Pacific and the shifting of US Navy assets to the region to account for fully 60 percent of all US naval strength.[6]

In response, Beijing claimed the entire South China Sea as its territorial waters and a "core national interest."[7] Reports and eventually video trickled out of People's Liberation Army (PLA) Navy ships harassing US Navy ships operating in the South China Sea on various occasions, raising memories of the March 2001 collision between a US Navy surveillance plane and a Chinese fighter jet, caused by the reckless flying on the part of the Chinese pilot, who died in the incident.[8]

When Washington failed to support Manila during the Scarborough Shoal crisis of mid-2012, allowing China to take effective control of the shoal, Beijing felt assured that US commitments to support allies in the South China Sea were hollow. New Chinese leader Xi Jinping added more concrete action to rhetoric, staging seemingly uncoordinated encounters once he came to power in late 2012. Starting around 2013, despite the Obama administration's continuing high-level bilateral meetings, the PRC began a major land-reclamation campaign in the Spratlys and then proceeded to militarize its new possessions, as well as some older ones in the Paracels.[9] The Chinese military built three Pearl Harbor–size port facilities, laid runways capable of handling fighter jets and bombers, installed radar and antiship and antiaircraft weapons, and built barracks and storage facilities, among other actions. The emplacement of airfields and weaponry on its claimed possessions gave Beijing the ability to effectively control the heart of the South China Sea, through which as much as 70 percent of global trade passed, and to project power throughout the region. It also launched its first aircraft carrier and conducted military exercises hundreds of miles from its recognized territorial waters, near the strategic waterways of Southeast Asian nations. PLA Navy (PLAN) ships regularly transited into the Indian Ocean and through strategic straits near Japan into the western Pacific Ocean.

The Obama administration's response to these Chinese moves was muddled and hesitant. It initially downplayed the island-building campaign, then condemned it, belatedly demanding that Beijing cease its actions, in response to which Chinese officials darkly warned of war should the United States not stop its pressure campaign. Washington also failed to take advantage of international law in its response to Beijing, even after The Hague's Permanent Court of Arbitration ruled in July 2016 against Chinese claims in a case brought by the Philippines.[10] Declaring that Beijing could not assert ownership over low-elevation landforms, even if they had been built up, and that it had no standing for its historical claims in the South China Sea, The Hague's court should have been a deterrent to China's course. Beijing, however, simply ignored the court's ruling, and the Obama administration did nothing to rally regional pressure on China.

Most noticeably, Obama hesitated to conduct military operations in the contested area, which would have sent clear signals to Beijing that the United States would not meekly surrender the area to China. It took the administration months to decide on freedom of navigation operations (FONOPS) that would come within twelve nautical miles of China's new islands, the territorial limit for legitimate possessions. Only four FONOPS were conducted during Obama's last two years in office, and the US Navy muddied the waters by claiming that it was conducting "innocent passage," which is a different category of transit under international law.[11] Chinese ships and aircraft did not actively interfere with American forces during these operations but instead shadowed them, issuing repeated warnings to leave the area. The end result of Obama's approach was to make the United States appear irresolute and confused about how to blunt China's advances. It further raised doubts in the minds of Asian allies, especially the Philippines, about whether Washington would live up to its treaty commitments.

Donald Trump became president having taken perhaps the hardest line of any presidential candidate toward China. Rejecting prior presidential approaches, Trump explicitly linked trade and security issues, promising to end China's unfair trading practices and warning that he would challenge Beijing in the South

China Sea. After his first few months in office, when it appeared that he would revert to a more traditional posture toward China, Trump levied major tariffs against Chinese goods, ultimately encompassing $550 billion, or nearly all of China's exports to the United States. At the same time, he increased military spending and authorized more FONOPS and aerial overflights in the South China Sea, ultimately increasing them to approximately one every three weeks by the beginning of 2025. Trump's approach was codified in the December 2017 National Security Strategy, which labeled China a "revisionist power" seeking to "displace the United States in the Indo-Pacific region . . . and reorder the region in its favor."[12] Openly acknowledging the strategic competition with China, the Trump administration targeted Chinese technology companies, mused about restricting the numbers of Chinese students in American universities, and sought a decoupling of the two countries' intertwined economies.

Through these years, tensions between Washington and Beijing rose dramatically, and multiple unsafe encounters occurred between the forces of the two nations, always instigated by PLAN ships or Air Force planes. Xi Jinping, who was chairman of the Central Military Commission in addition to being general secretary of the Chinese Communist Party (CCP) and president, had told his military as far back as 2018 to "prepare for war," and his exhortations against American interference in China's "rightful" sphere of interest increased over the succeeding years, leading to risk-taking actions on the part of Chinese sailors and pilots.[13] While high-level bilateral diplomatic meetings continued to take place, they resulted in no solutions to the festering problems, and both sides recognized that such gatherings were increasingly for show. Beijing attempted to use Chinese students studying in US universities to whip up pro-Chinese sentiment on campuses and in major US cities, but the efforts backfired after a few student ringleaders revealed the Chinese government's organizing role. While the vast majority of Chinese Americans supported Washington, some activists, likely plants from China, vocally urged concessions to Beijing, using social media to spread their message.

Meanwhile, US allies in Asia sought to prevent an outright breach between the two giant nations, but at the same time saw advantages in having both Beijing and Washington attempt to curry favor with them, whether through lessening demands on them, offering trade blandishments, or elevating diplomatic exchanges.

All this took its inevitable toll on the publics of both nations. At the 20th National Party Congress of the Chinese Communist Party, in November 2022, Xi stayed on as paramount leader, which was widely expected, and inserted a plank seen as a preemptive declaration that China would seek hegemony over the South China Sea by 2049. Public opinion polls taken in 2024 showed that the number of respondents in China and the United States having a positive opinion of the other country had dropped to single digits and that each considered the other its number one potential adversary. In short, the political relationship between the United States and China had deteriorated to such a degree by 2025 that relations seemed nearly unsalvageable.

THE ANTEBELLUM MILITARY BALANCE

As relations worsened, military planners in both countries stepped up their contingency and operational planning. While few professional military officers believed they would face the other side in actual combat, their responsibility lay in ensuring that their political leaders had the most complete set of military options available and that their forces were trained and equipped for potential conflict.

The subsequent events of the war depended in large part on the military balance that held between the two at the outbreak of hostilities. For the United States, it was the first time it had conducted large-scale military operations in Asia in a half century, since the end of the Vietnam War. For the PRC, its last full-scale conflicts had been the 1962 Sino-Indian War and the shorter but intense 1979 border war with Vietnam. Yet despite rhetoric about becoming a global power, Beijing had focused its military development on being able to conduct regional operations and control both sea and sky space for extended periods of time, within the so-called first and second island chains, encompassing the Yellow, East China, and South China Seas.[14] This allowed a concentration of forces at strategic points in the regional theater, generated from continental bases and on Hainan Island in the South China Sea, and with access to Chinese bases in both the Spratly and Paracel island chains in the same sea.

Chinese doctrine had steadily moved toward a more prominent role for naval, air, rocket, and strategic forces. The PLAN had increased its number of surface and subsurface vessels and fielded two aircraft carriers (but only one fully outfitted for naval operations), twenty-six destroyers equipped with Aegis-like antiair systems or advanced radar arrays, and thirty smaller ships, along with fifty attack submarines, almost all conventionally powered.[15] The combined PLAN Air Force (PLANAF) and PLA Air Force (PLAAF) boasted more than 100 J-31 and J-20 advanced fighters with stealth features, in addition to 600 fourth-generation fighters, primarily J-10, J-11, and J-15 carrier variants.[16] China's first, understrength squadron of H-20 long-range stealth bombers also entered service in 2025, putting at risk American bases in Guam and as far as Hawaii. Beijing also deployed more than 1,000 short-range ballistic missiles with ranges up to 1,000 kilometers, and 250 medium-range missiles that could reach targets 3,000 kilometers away. Central to its missile force was the DF-21D antiship ballistic missile, which boasted a range of 1,500 kilometers and included maneuverable reentry vehicle warheads that could autonomously track targets, and the intermediate-range DF-26, with a range of 3,000 to 5,400 kilometers.[17]

With the world's largest defense budget and decades of forward deployment throughout the world, the US military appeared to have the edge over any potential competitor. Though on paper it seemed to have no peer, its force was aging, and it had not yet recapitalized some of its major systems. As an expeditionary force, the US military appeared postured to respond quickly to any conflict, but as would be shown, it lacked the depth to maintain a long campaign. The US Pacific Fleet provided the main naval presence in the region, composed of the US Third and Seventh Fleets. With the USS *Gerald R. Ford* (CVN 78), the US Navy's newest aircraft carrier, homeported in Yokosuka, Japan, the US Seventh Fleet had 22 ships in Asian waters—including 2 cruisers, 8 guided-missile destroyers (DDGs), 4 nuclear-powered attack submarines, and an amphibious assault ship—with another 40 available based in Hawaii and the Pacific Coast of the United States.[18] Third Fleet forces, drawn from California, Washington, and Hawaii, provided the potential of another 2 active carriers, with 140 airplanes and 10 more submarines.[19] The continental-based US naval forces faced a two-week transit to Japan and three weeks to the Strait of Malacca, while those in Hawaii were a week away from US bases in Japan. Added to the naval forces were the airplanes of the Pacific Air Forces, based at Anderson Air Force Base in Guam and Kadena, Yokota, and Misawa air bases in Japan (the South Korea–based air force squadrons remained detailed for peninsular defense). These roughly three hundred aircraft included two squadrons of F-35s and F-22s, with the remainder being older F-15s and F-16s.[20]

THE GRAY RHINO: SEPTEMBER 8–9, 2025

The Littoral War began with a series of accidental encounters in the skies and waters near Scarborough Shoal, in the South China Sea.[21] Beijing had effectively taken control of the shoal, long a point of contention between China and the Philippines, in 2012.[22] After Philippines president Rodrigo Duterte, who had steadily moved Manila toward China during the late 2010s, was impeached and removed from office, the Philippines' new president moved to reassert Manila's claim to the shoal, including sending coastal patrol boats into waters near the contested territory during the summer of 2025. When armed People's Armed Forces Maritime Militia (PAFMM) vessels pushed out the Filipino forces in early

July, Manila appealed to Washington under its security treaty for assistance.[23]

Prior Philippine requests for US help in dealing with China had been largely shunted aside by Washington, even during the Trump administration. However, new US president Gavin Newsom, who had been dogged during the 2024 campaign by allegations that Chinese cyber operations had benefited his candidacy, saw the Philippine request as an opportunity to show his willingness to take a hard line against Beijing. Newsom increased US Air Force flights over the contested territory, using air bases made available by Manila, and sent the *Gerald Ford*, along with escort vessels, on a short transit. On two occasions in late July, US and Chinese ships came close to running into each other due to aggressive PLAN maneuvering, and a US Navy FA-18 operating from the *Gerald Ford* was forced to take emergency evasive action to avoid colliding with a PLANAF J-15.[24] Despite the increasing tensions, the US Navy ships returned to Japan at the beginning of August, yet no diplomatic attempts were made to alter the trajectory of events. The fact that both sides knew some type of armed encounter was increasingly possible, if not probable, yet seemed to ignore the risk, led pundits to call the events surrounding the clash an example of a "gray rhino," unlike the complete surprise represented by a "black swan" occurrence. Ironically, Xi Jinping himself had warned about the dangers of "gray rhinos" back in 2018 and 2019.[25]

In response to the brief uptick in US Navy FONOPS near other Chinese-claimed territory in the Spratly and Paracel island chains, Beijing decided to fortify Scarborough Shoal, building airstrips and naval facilities as it had done in the Spratlys. As Scarborough lay only 140 miles from Manila, China's announcement set off alarm bells in the Philippines.[26] As Chinese naval construction ships approached Scarborough on September 4, dozens of small Philippine boats, many of them private, attempted to block them. On the second day of the maritime encounter, a Chinese frigate rammed a Philippine fishing boat, sinking it, with the loss of two seamen.[27] As news spread over the next several days, dozens more Philippine vessels, including the country's entire coast guard, confronted the Chinese. Though no further ship collisions occurred, worldwide broadcast of video of the maritime confrontation further inflamed tensions.

At this point, on Saturday, September 6, US Indo-Pacific Command, acting directly under orders from US secretary of defense Michèle Flournoy, dispatched one guided missile destroyer, the USS *Curtis Wilbur* (DDG 54), and the *Independence*-class littoral combat ship the USS *Charleston* (LCS 18) to the waters off Scarborough, and ordered the USS *John C. Stennis* (CVN 74) aircraft carrier to head from its home port in Bremerton, Washington, to Pearl Harbor.[28] In order not to inflame the high tensions, however, the White House and Pentagon decided not to send its Japan-based aircraft carrier, the USS *Gerald Ford*, to the area. Instead, another US guided-missile destroyer, USS *Stethem* (DDG 63), and a mine countermeasures ship, the USS *Patriot* (MCM 7), were ordered to transit the Taiwan Strait. The next day, Beijing announced an air defense identification zone over the entire South China Sea, demanding that all non-Chinese aircraft submit their flight plans to Chinese military authorities and receive clearance to proceed.[29] While the US Air Force and Navy immediately rejected China's authority over the South China Sea, PLAAF and PLANAF aerial patrols increased, and international civilian airliners complied with Beijing's demands.

On Monday, September 8, at approximately 18:30 local time (10:30 Greenwich time; 00:30 Hawaii time; 05:30 eastern time), a US Navy EP-3 surveillance flight out of Japan over the Spratlys was intercepted by a PLAAF J-20 taking off from Fiery Cross Reef, in the same chain. After warning off the EP-3, the J-20 attempted a barrel roll over the American plane. The Chinese pilot sheared off most of the EP-3's tail and left rear stabilizer; the Chinese plane lost a wing and went into an unrecoverable spin into the sea. The EP-3 also could not recover and plunged into the sea, killing all twenty-two Americans aboard.[30] Tragically, the EP-3 was not even supposed to be flying, as the US Navy had intended to replace the

fleet with unmanned surveillance drones by 2020, but cost over-
runs and delays in the drone program led to occasional use of a
limited number of aging manned aircraft in the region, especially
when real-time interpretation of data was required.[31]

Roughly thirty minutes later, before word of the EP-3's down-
ing had reached US Indo-Pacific Command in Hawaii, let alone
Washington or Beijing, 13 nm northwest of Scarborough Shoal,
the *Bertholf* (WMSL 750), a US Coast Guard cutter returning from
a training mission along with the Japan Coast Guard *Kunigami*-
class patrol vessel *Motobu* (PL-13), out of Naha in Okinawa, was
approached by a cutter-class armed Chinese Coast Guard (CCG)
ship. After broadcasting warnings for the *Bertholf* and the *Motobu*
to leave the area, the Chinese ship attempted to maneuver in front
of the American ship, to turn its bow.[32] The CCG captain miscalculated and struck the *Bertholf* amidships, caving in the mess and
one of its enlisted crew compartments. The *Bertholf* began taking
on water and attempted to turn east toward the Philippines while
emergency crews attempted to keep the ship afloat. The CCG ship
immediately left the scene without rendering assistance. Six US
sailors later were declared missing and presumed dead in the collision, while three Chinese CCG sailors were swept overboard
and lost at sea.

Being the closest US naval vessel to the downed EP-3, the *Curtis Wilbur* raced toward the site of its crash, while the *Charleston*
moved to assist the *Bertholf*. Nighttime darkness caused confusion
for rescue and patrol operations on both sides. Two PLAN ships
returned to the scene of the maritime collision to search for the
lost Chinese seamen, coming in close quarters with the *Motobu*—
which was helping in rescue operations to stabilize the American
vessel—as well as with the littoral combat ship *Charleston*, which
arrived several hours later. Mechanical trouble kept the *Bertholf*
from making way under her own power, and she began to drift
back toward PLAN vessels In the darkness, US ships and the
Japanese attempted to disengage with the Chinese vessels, while
continually warning the other side to stand down so rescue operations could continue.

After several close encounters, one Type 052D Luyang III-class PLAN destroyer, the *Taiyuan* (131), activated its fire-control radar and locked on the *Motobu*.[33] The captain of the thousand-ton Japanese patrol ship, knowing he could not survive a direct hit from the PLAN destroyer, radioed repeated demands that the radar be turned off. When no Chinese response was forthcoming, and with rescue operations ongoing, the *Motobu*'s commander fired one round from his Bushmaster II 30 mm chain gun across the bow of the *Taiyuan*. In response, a nearby Chinese frigate, thinking it was under attack from the Japanese Coast Guard ship, fired a torpedo in the direction of the *Motobu*. In the congested seas, however, the torpedo hit the *Charleston*, which was transiting between the Chinese and Japanese ships, ripping a hole below the waterline. The lightly armored littoral combat ship, with a complement of fifty officers and seamen, foundered in just twenty-five minutes, with an unknown loss of life, at 01:30 (17:30 Greenwich time; 07:30 Hawaii time; 10:30 eastern time) on Tuesday, September 9.[34] US surveillance drones flying over the melee recorded parts of the encounter and flashed images back to US commanders in the region.

THE CHOICE FOR WAR: SEPTEMBER 9–23, 2025

When word of the aerial and maritime encounters began filtering in to the USS *Blue Ridge* (LCC 19), flagship of the US Navy's Seventh Fleet, and US Pacific Fleet headquarters in Hawaii, rescue operations were immediately ordered. As the late-night and early-morning melee developed, US commanders watched in near real time as the *Charleston* sank. Within ten minutes, the *Curtis Wilbur* was ordered to leave the site of the downed EP-3 and instead move to pick up all US survivors from the two lost ships. Within twenty minutes, the four-star admiral in command of US Indo-Pacific Command had directed the commander of the US Pacific Fleet to order the *Gerald Ford* to steam to the location, provide rescue operations, and protect all US and allied ships in the South China Sea area. Over the previous decade, as Chinese naval and missile capabilities increased, it became a working assumption that US carriers would be kept out of the "kill zone" of Chinese missiles and submarines in the case of any hostilities. However, with the loss of American lives, the White House ordered the Pentagon to send the *Gerald Ford* as a message to Beijing. This tactical decision would have strategic consequences in the coming weeks.

It would take two days to get underway and seven days total for the *Gerald Ford* to reach the scene; in the meantime, only one US ship, the *Curtis Wilbur*, was in the waters of the accident, as the USS *Wasp* (LHD 1), an amphibious assault ship that carried ten US Marine Corps F-35s, was paying a port visit to Chennai, India, for a series of scheduled naval exercises with the Indian Navy.

US forces needed air protection, but with the *Gerald Ford* days away, the commander of US Indo-Pacific Command ordered US Pacific Air Forces to scramble four F-35As to the South China Sea from Kadena Air Force Base in Okinawa, a distance of approximately 920 nm (the F-22 Raptor's combat radius of 490 nm was deemed insufficient for the mission). The F-35s would then be deployed to Clark Air Base in the Philippines, to allow for longer-duration operations in the area. With a combat radius of 669 nm, the F-35 required refueling, and the mission was delayed until KC-46A tankers reached approximately halfway stationing points northwest of Luzon Island in the Philippines. After reaching the patrol station in the early afternoon of September 9, the F-35s encountered two PLAAF J-20 fighters launched from Fiery Cross Reef.[35] The Chinese radioed for backup, and two more J-20s soon arrived. After ten minutes of shadowing each other with repeated calls from each side for the other to withdraw, one of the Chinese jets attempted another close encounter head on, clipping the wing of one F-35. Both pilots were forced to eject, and almost simultaneously, a second J-20 launched an air-to-air missile at one of the remaining F-35s. At this point, the American pilots, who had received permission to defend themselves if fired upon, targeted and destroyed the three remaining J-20s, but not before one J-20 destroyed another F-35, with the loss of the American pilot. When the Chinese learned about the aerial encounter, the PLA chief of staff recommended missile attacks on US air bases in Okinawa; this, however, was vetoed by Xi Jinping, in his role as chairman of the Central Military Commission (CMC). While American war planners did not know of Xi's decision, they anticipated the horizontal escalation of hostilities to US bases in the region and were surprised at the lack of enemy action against them.[36] For many Chinese postconflict commentators, Xi's decision not to attack Japan in the earliest stages of the conflict was a strategic error that prevented complete victory.

At this point, as intelligence about the aerial dogfight streamed into the US Pacific Fleet's Maritime Operations Center, the Pac-Fleet commander sent orders to the US Seventh Fleet commander for the *Curtis Wilbur* to defend the *Bertholf* and disable any Chinese ship that interfered with ongoing rescue and repair operations. Similar orders went out to Pacific Air Forces to maintain steady air cover and intercept any Chinese fighter jets from entering a twenty-mile radius of the accident site. At the same time, he issued orders for all mission-ready Seventh Fleet combat forces to steam from Yokosuka, Japan, at full speed toward the Spratlys. This consisted of one cruiser, the USS *Antietam* (CG 54), and three *Arleigh Burke*-class destroyers, making roughly twenty knots; in addition, a nearby nuclear-powered attack submarine was diverted to lurk in the waters near Scarborough Shoal. However, given that the additional US forces would not reach the Spratlys for close to a week, while the *Wasp* began the trip back from India, US firepower was limited to the *Curtis Wilbur*, with the ship taking up a visible position near Scarborough Shoal and the site of the clashes. To intimidate the Chinese, B-52s based in Guam commenced regular overflights of Chinese bases in the Spratlys on Wednesday, September 10.[37]

The American response was designed to sanitize the immediate area of the clash, but not to widen the theater of operations or prevent Chinese ships and planes from transiting the South China Sea, except for the area where the Americans were concentrating on rescue operations. This "minimum deterrence" approach made political sense but ultimately created opportunities for Beijing to take military advantage of US hesitancy.[38] President Newsom had been informed within minutes of the sinking of the *Charleston* and, eager to dispel lingering rumors that he was beholden to China for his electoral victory, confirmed the operational plans of Indo-Pacific Command issued on September 9, while approving further deployments of a second aircraft carrier, the *John C. Stennis*, and three more destroyers from Hawaii to the South China Sea, along with three nuclear attack submarines (SSNs), including the USS *Illinois* (SSN 786), from Submarine Group 7 in Guam to positions off the Strait of Malacca, the Paracel Islands, and Hainan Island. After making this decision, President Newsom went on national television to brief the nation, promising that he would protect American interests and never back down from America's role in the Pacific.

The Failure of Diplomacy

An urgent phone call between President Newsom and Chairman Xi that evening did little to stabilize the situation, and on the evening of September 10, Beijing time, a doctored video of the ramming of the *Bertholf* was spread in China that made it look like the Americans were to blame for the accident. Chinese internet censors allowed the clip to become a viral sensation, and stage-managed crowds soon thronged the gates of the American and Japanese embassies, shouting slogans denouncing the United States and Japan, throwing stones and trash onto the grounds, and demanding compensation from Washington and Tokyo.[39] Xi took to the airwaves to chastise the Americans, but also to try to rise above the fray, announcing that China would not further deepen the crisis. This tactic backfired, and crowds began moving toward Tiananmen Square, demanding that China push America out of Asia, while the internet lit up with criticism of Xi that questioned his mental state. Chinese overseas students and provocateurs under guidance from the CCP's United Front Work Department propaganda unit began coordinated protests in Sydney, Seoul, London, Paris, Toronto, and Vancouver, while small groups of Chinese students at US universities, including Harvard, Columbia, UC Berkeley, and UCLA, staged demonstrations that garnered widespread media coverage.[40]

At an emergency meeting of the Chinese Communist Party's Standing Committee and then the Central Military Commission (CMC) on September 11, Xi reversed his previously cautious course. He ordered the PLAN to block all US ships from coming into China's "historic waters" of the South China Sea, and to either escort out or capture any US vessels remaining in the sea. He also ordered a no-fly zone over the Spratlys and Paracels. Moreover, he promised to target any Japanese naval ships that accompanied US vessels into the South China Sea. However, Xi continued to reject suggestions that US air bases in Japan, or Japanese air bases, immediately be targeted with ballistic missiles, a decision that caused deep resentment within the PLA.

China's Choice to Expand the War

Nonetheless, Xi's decision to confront US forces and essentially turn a skirmish into a war has been hotly debated by historians. Without access to the papers of the Standing Committee or CMC, and with diplomatic and academic ties between China and the United States severely curtailed after the war, it is largely guesswork as to why Xi chose the path he did. Some analysts point to the weakness of the Chinese economy, which had resulted in growing public dissatisfaction for several years, and surmise that the war was a way to divert public attention. Others argue that shrinking military budgets, which were used by China's political adversaries in Asia to claim that its days as the most powerful Asian military were drawing to a close, caused fear among China's top leadership that their military strength was a wasting asset. Many, however, argue that Beijing's grand strategy had been clear for years, underscoring Xi's belligerent rhetoric stretching back to the 2010s and his assertion that Taiwan would be absorbed into China, as evidence that he was waiting for an opportunity to give a black eye to an America he believed was unwilling to put up a major fight.[41] Whatever the actual reason, it seems clear that Chinese leaders, above all Xi, realized they had just a few days to try to stake out a dominant position before US Navy vessels began reaching the Spratlys and reinforcements from San Diego reached Yokosuka. At the same time, though, Xi and his top lieutenants sought initially to avoid the unrestrained use of asymmetric tactics, such as cyberattacks, which could escalate into a clash involving both homelands. Orders appear to have gone out on September 11 for two task forces to make steam, for air forces to begin combat patrols, and for a diversionary fleet in the north.

- From the East Sea Fleet based at Ningbo, four diesel attack submarines, three Type 052D destroyers, nine frigates, two amphibious helicopter carriers, and ten missile patrol craft were dispatched toward the Senkaku/Diaoyu Islands northeast of Taiwan. Their orders were to block any US and Japanese vessels from transiting south of Taiwan into the South China Sea. They were accompanied by twenty armed CCG ships ordered to invade Japan's territorial waters in the Senkakus and thereby draw off Japanese ships.
- The *Liaoning*, China's aircraft carrier, and a small escort group from the East Sea Fleet were sent toward Luzon, in the Philippines, to block the *Gerald Ford* from reaching the South China Sea.
- From the South Sea Fleet based at Zhanjiang, three diesel attack submarines, three Type 052D destroyers, seven frigates, twelve missile patrol craft, and three corvettes were dispatched to the Spratlys. Their mission was to surround and immobilize the *Curtis Wilbur* and the crippled *Bertholf*. Two other diesel attack submarines were sent toward the Strait of Malacca to close passage through to the Indian Ocean, if necessary.
- To prevent the United States from maintaining air cover for its ships, PLAN Type 052D destroyers armed with advanced HQ-9 surface-to-air missiles (SAMs) were ordered to engage any US Navy or Air Force fighters, while Chinese air forces, including the PLAAF and land-based PLANAF fighters, were ordered to make combat air patrols over the Spratlys; US Air Force tankers were to

be targeted off Luzon, so as to make Japan-based fighter coverage impossible.

- As a diversionary tactic, the North Sea Fleet, out of Qingdao, dispatched a flotilla of destroyers, frigates, and corvettes into the East China Sea, toward the Jeju and Korean Straits, hoping to draw off Japan Maritime Self-Defense Force ships (JMSDF) from supporting the US Navy.

The Taiwan Strait Is Lost

First blood in the expanded theater of operations was drawn by the Chinese on September 12. The USS *Stethem* and USS *Patriot*, previously ordered to transit the Taiwan Strait, were caught in a swarm of Chinese fishing craft, Type 22 PLAN missile patrol boats, and Chinese Coast Guard ships that had crossed the median line at a point about halfway through the strait. Slowed to a crawl by the swarm of small craft and alarmed by the threatening tactics from the boats, the *Stethem* felt forced to fire warning shots. This resulted in a missile swarm fired from the small PLAN patrol craft, which apparently had orders to attack the US ships if they gave any justification for doing so, such as firing their guns even in defense. The *Patriot* sustained casualties and serious damage, and the *Stethem*, while also sustaining damage, returned fire, disabling one of the CCG ships and several of the missile boats, and driving off the others. US Air Force F-22s operating out of Kadena (approximately 400 nm away) engaged with older Chinese J-10s and J-11s, which had been sent to harass the American vessels, destroying eight planes before breaking off. The *Stethem* and *Patriot* eventually broke free of the swarm and limped to Kaohsiung, Taiwan. This allowed Beijing to claim on September 13 that Taiwan was now a belligerent and to announce that the Taiwan Strait was closed, send a blockading force to Kaohsiung just outside Taiwan's twelve-mile territorial limit, position two more Type 052D destroyers for antiair missions over the Taiwan Strait, and begin multiple combat aerial patrols around the island. Taiwanese naval ships sent to meet the Chinese were stopped just inside the territorial limit, and the two navies settled for the moment into a watchful stalemate.

The next three days slowed to a dead calm in the region as the various task forces and ships of both sides neared each other. Neither Newsom nor Xi was willing to declare war on the other country, with all the implications that held, but Xi declared a national emergency, and Newsom briefed congressional leaders, who quickly passed a nonbinding resolution declaring support for US forces in Asia and for President Newsom's policy of maintaining a "peaceful and prosperous Indo-Pacific." Despite repeated phone calls between the leaders, neither agreed to pull back forces. Instead, Newsom approved the dispatch to Japan of ten more DDGs and two cruisers from San Diego, though their transit would take at least two weeks. Another two squadrons of F-22s were ordered to Kadena, and two B-2 bombers from Whiteman Air Force Base made a transoceanic flyby over the Senkakus. When Newsom asked for permission to base the F-22s at Clark, widespread anti-US protests broke out in the Philippines, including massive demonstrations that besieged the base; these were organized and directed by Chinese intelligence agents, but they served to paralyze Philippine politics, especially once former president Duterte emerged at the head of the protestors demanding that Manila restore peaceful relations with Beijing.

On September 15, the PLAN South Sea Fleet task force reached the position of the *Curtis Wilbur*, off the Spratlys. The *Bertholf* remained largely inoperable, and the DDG kept watch over the Coast Guard vessel. Despite warnings to keep a safe maritime distance, the Chinese ships closed in, forcing the DDG to fire warning shots, which were ignored. Being entirely outgunned, the commander of the *Curtis Wilbur* chose to batten down the ship and refrain from further hostilities, hoping to ride out any Chinese attack until relief forces could arrive; the Chinese, who had orders only to isolate the two American ships, formed a barrier around them. In the skies, US tankers had been withdrawn from their refueling stations, as Pacific Air Forces feared losing its limited number of them due to PLA fighters, while the Philippines' president refused permission for further US air operations to be flown from Clark; this effectively ended US fighter support over the South China Sea.

The Battle of Bashi Channel

The next day, September 16, the aircraft carrier *Liaoning*, which was approximately 175 nm northwest of the Babuyan Islands, just north of Luzon, launched a combination of J-31 and J-15 jets to try to intimidate the *Gerald Ford*, which was to the southeast of Okinawa, approximately 75 nm northeast of the Philippines' Batanes, in the western Pacific Ocean. The geography of eastern Asia's inner seas meant that the most direct route to intercept the American ships would have forced the Chinese to transit past the Japanese-held Ryukyu Islands, making them vulnerable to land-based jets from Okinawa as well as potential antiship missiles launched from islands along the chain. The PLAN vessels instead swung south through the Taiwan Strait, running the risk of encountering lurking US submarines, and then northeast to the Bashi Channel. Nonetheless, the Chinese planes were decisively defeated by a combination of the *Gerald Ford*'s F-35s and F-22s launched from Kadena, on Okinawa, effectively preventing the *Liaoning* and its flotilla from moving forward. However, one Type 055D PLAN destroyer, its newest variant, escorting the *Liaoning* used its HQ-9 SAMs to destroy one F-35 and one F-22, underscoring the danger to US fighters. At the same time, the US escort ships also halted just within visual range of East Sea Fleet vessels on the horizon.

At this point, the clashes threatened to involve land-based forces, which would have escalated the war to a higher, and possibly uncontrollable, level. US Pacific Fleet anticipated the employment of DF-21D antiship ballistic missiles against the *Gerald Ford*, and indeed two missiles were launched from Chinese territory approximately four hours after the aerial engagement. The Americans countered with antimissile SM-6s to knock down the DF-21Ds, which failed; however, both Chinese missiles also missed the *Gerald Ford*. Some in Washington chose to believe the failed missile attack was purposeful, with Beijing trying to send a message that it would knock out the US carrier were it to continue on into the South China Sea. However, in the press of time, voices arguing that Washington needed to send a signal back to Beijing were dismissed. Instead, within three hours of the attempted DF-21 strike, orders came from Hawaii, originating in Washington, that the *Gerald Ford* was to hold position east of the Bashi Channel, located 100 miles north of Luzon and 120 miles south of Taiwan, which essentially formed the border between the Philippine and South China Seas. Now the strategic implications of sending US aircraft carriers into Beijing's "kill zone" were becoming clear. Washington planners were in a quandary, for the *Gerald Ford* remained within range of both DF-21D and DF-26 missiles, but officials were loath to pull the carrier farther back, for fear of being seen as abandoning the conflict; nor did they want to risk an escalation of hostilities by targeting Chinese assets not directly involved in the skirmishing. Again, it appeared that the Chinese had checked the Americans, though without knocking them off the board.

When word reached Taiwan that the *Gerald Ford* had halted, the island's president, from the mainland-leaning Kuomintang (KMT) party, announced on September 17 that Taiwan was henceforth a neutral in the conflict and would accept Chinese naval patrols of its sea-lanes and overflight. He further ordered the two US ships that had taken refuge there to either leave Taiwanese waters or declare they were no longer combatants and remain quarantined in port.

The Chinese Introduce Electronic Warfare

After one day on station, on September 17, the escort ships with the *Gerald Ford*, including the cruiser *Antietam* and three DDGs, continued toward the Spratlys. The PLA Strategic Support Force then began wide-scale electronic warfare measures and cyberattacks on US systems, after hesitant moves to interrupt US systems in the first week of the conflict. It succeeded in repeatedly interrupting GPS and shutting down various US computer and communications systems, including intelligence, surveillance, and reconnaissance (ISR) feeds, through malware. US EA-18G Growler electronic warfare aircraft launched from the *Gerald Ford* and EP-3s from Japan also found their systems jammed, leaving US commanders reliant on incomplete information from satellites and submarines. This significantly slowed the progress of the US flotilla toward the Spratlys and was only partially countered by launching dozens of line-of-sight communications transmitters tethered to medium-altitude balloons from US Navy ships scattered throughout the theater of operations. With the advent of electronic warfare, US policy makers began to fear that a future wave of cyberattacks would widen the field of conflict to civilian systems, forcing a major US response. For the time being, however, the Chinese hesitated to escalate the crisis horizontally by targeting noncombatants, focusing instead on crippling US operations in the theater of combat.

The Battle of Santiago Island

On September 20, the US flotilla engaged in hostilities with the South Sea Fleet off Santiago Island, near the town of Bolinao on Luzon. The *Gerald Ford* sent F-18s and F-35s for air cover, easily shooting down PLAAF and PLANAF planes from the Spratlys; given the roughly 600-mile distance from PLANAF bases on Hainan Island and PLAAF bases near Guangzhou, and the lack of in-flight aerial refueling, the Chinese were limited to just the three dozen or so fighters on various Spratly bases. Once again, however, HQ-9s launched from Type 052Ds scored hits on US planes, destroying three F-18s. From nearly 100 nm away, two Chinese Type 052C destroyers loosed a volley of six antiship missiles, which scored hits on the *Antietam* and one DDG, disabling both. US naval forces returned fire, sinking one Chinese destroyer and inflicting serious damage on another. The remaining two US DDGs then endured the missile volleys of ten Type 22 missile boats, each of which fired its complement of eight antiship subsonic cruise missiles. While five of the ten Chinese missile boats were destroyed by return American fire, one remaining US DDG was sunk and the other disabled. The US flotilla from Japan had been stopped several hundred miles north of the Spratlys and the US ships involved in the original melee of September 9. The Chinese then boarded the *Curtis Wilbur* early on the morning of September 21 and scuttled the *Bertholf*, transferring all US military personnel to Mischief Reef for internment. This was a total of 415 sailors and Coast Guard members, including several dozen seriously wounded.

The Battle of the Senkakus

On September 21–22, Japanese Coast Guard and Japan Maritime Self-Defense Force ships engaged with elements of the PLAN's East Sea Fleet and the People's Armed Forces Maritime Militia (PAFMM). Though PAFMM vessels had reached the Senkakus on September 14, the East Sea Fleet did not release ships to the mission until September 18, after making sure that the *Gerald Ford* had halted at the Batanes in the Bashi Channel. It was, in fact, the sailing away of several East Sea Fleet vessels toward the Senkakus that led the *Gerald Ford*'s escort vessels to continue south toward Santiago Island.

Japanese Coast Guard (JCG) ships had played cat and mouse with PAFMM ships since September 14 in the waters off the Senkakus, but with the arrival of the PLAN ships already on patrol in the East China Sea, the PAFMM vessels boldly moved within two miles or so of the islands. An interdiction by the Japanese turned into a skirmish, but the much heavier-armed PAFMM vessel sank the one thousand-ton JCG cutter, with the loss of ten Coast Guard members. An emergency call was answered by JASDF F-2 fighters, which had been moved to Kadena specifically for antiship missions. The F-2s launched SAM-2 antiship missiles that disabled two PAFMM ships. Three hours later, fighters launched from the *Liaoning*, which had moved north from its position near the Babuyan Islands into the Bashi Channel between the Batanes and Taiwan. These J-15s successfully attacked four JCG cutters with standoff air-to-surface missiles, sinking or disabling them.

With JMSDF ships en route to the Senkakus but not yet off station, the JCG withdrew its remaining ships toward Okinawa, leaving the islands undefended except for fighters based at New Ishigaki Airport, which was converted to military use.

The Japanese had another card to play, however, and in the early morning hours of September 22, the *Shoryu* (SS-510), a *Soryu*-class diesel-electric attack submarine that had been lurking southwest of the Senkakus, intercepted the *Liaoning* and loosed four Type 89 guided torpedoes, two of which struck the Chinese aircraft carrier below the waterline. The *Liaoning* was halted and began to list, at which point the *Shoryu* surfaced and launched six Harpoon missiles, four of which found their target, leaving the *Liaoning* out of commission and severely listing to port. Four Chinese attack submarines that had been in Taiwanese waters then hunted down the *Shoryu*, sinking her with all sixty-five hands on board just before midnight on September 23, southeast of Okinawa, where she was making a run for sanctuary.

When intelligence of the disabling of the *Liaoning* reached East Sea Fleet headquarters at Ningbo, the assumption was made that an American submarine had attacked the carrier. In response, orders went out to retaliate by targeting the *Gerald Ford*, which had turned north from the Batanes after receiving word of the battle off the Senkakus. Again, the Chinese launched DF-21D anti-ship ballistic missiles; unlike on September 16, however, two missiles found their target after ineffective SM-6 countermeasures. The *Gerald Ford* sustained catastrophic damage and severe loss of life, and the ship foundered at nightfall. Japanese and American ships sent out from Okinawa reached the scene late on September 23 and commenced rescue operations, and the USS *John C. Stennis* hove into view the following day.

THE CHOICE FOR PEACE: SEPTEMBER 23–30, 2025

The successful attacks on the aircraft carriers of both nations were the turning point of the Littoral War. Senior policy makers in both countries realized they were now at the precipice of full-out conflict, where land-based targets and civilian populations could now be targeted. The US preference for containing the conflict in the global commons was at risk of being overtaken by events. Standard operating procedures at US Strategic Command, which controlled America's nuclear arsenal, had moved readiness on September 10 from peacetime Defense Condition (DEFCON) 5 to DEFCON 4, and then on September 12 to DEFCON 3, with enhanced readiness at underground missile silos and the ability to mobilize nuclear-armed bombers on ground alert. The PLA Rocket Force went to high alert on September 11, and a JIN-class nuclear ballistic missile submarine carrying the JL-2 submarine-launched ballistic missile sortied from its base at Longpo on Hainan Island, to join a counterpart already on patrol. When US Strategic Command obtained satellite imagery of the empty submarine wharves on Hainan on September 12, its commander ordered the USS *Louisiana* (SSBN 743) out of Bremerton, Washington, to join the USS *Kentucky* (SSBN 737), already on patrol in the Pacific.

After the Battle of the Senkakus, the expansion of the war to land-based, populated targets became the next logical military step, but one that US political and senior military leaders were loath to take. With the increase in readiness of strategic forces, use of nuclear force itself no longer seemed unthinkable, given the emotionalism likely to break out in both countries at the destruction of the aircraft carriers, the most visible symbols of their military power. More worrisome for operations planners in both countries was the likelihood that the Americans would begin targeting mobile DF-21D and DF-26 launchers on China's mainland to prevent the PLA from using any more antiship ballistic missiles. Such attacks would force the Chinese to begin attacking ground targets in response, possibly in Guam and even Hawaii, as well as in Japan, where US air and naval forces were based. Japanese policy makers braced themselves for a wave of Chinese ballistic missile attacks as a tactic to pressure Tokyo to abandon its American ally.

Unexpectedly, perhaps, the first steps toward a cessation of hostilities were proposed by the Chinese. The Chinese attack on the *Gerald Ford*, in mistaken retaliation for the *Liaoning* disabling, caused a rift in the Chinese leadership. CMC chairman Xi Jinping upbraided the East Sea Fleet leadership for not confirming that the Americans were behind the attack, a point made directly by President Newsom in a nationally televised address on September 23. Xi also concluded that an attack on another US carrier, the *John C. Stennis*, would likely lead the Americans to begin large-scale operations against Chinese land-based missile targets, docks, shipyards, and air bases. With more US ships reaching the theater of battle, it would be harder to control the conflict, and Beijing could wind up losing the gains it had made, namely eliminating the American presence in the South China Sea and taking control of the Taiwan Strait with a Finlandized Taiwan. Xi therefore contacted Newsom on the morning of September 23 and proposed an immediate cease-fire, to be followed by negotiations between military commanders for a permanent halt to combat operations.

Newsom faced a different set of constraints than Xi. With one aircraft carrier gone, the US Navy had only two fully operational carriers left from the total force of nine; it would take weeks to bring two more up to combat readiness and months to get another two ready for deployment. The navy had also deployed the majority of its combat-ready destroyers and submarines, and further losses from missile attacks would begin to seriously degrade the US capability to wage surface war. The US Air Force had outclassed its Chinese opponents, but its number of mission-ready airplanes was declining, as well as its stores of air-to-air missiles. Surging both naval and air units to the region left little in reserve for a longer conflict.

A grim balance had been achieved with the mirror attacks on the aircraft carriers, and Newsom responded positively to Xi's proposal, contingent on the immediate release of all US military personnel held by the Chinese, to which Xi consented, promising that they would be transferred to the Philippines by Chinese ships beginning on September 25. The two agreed that all combat operations would cease at 11:00 Beijing time on September 24, and forces would hold at their positions at the status quo.

The agreement could have been derailed just hours after the two leaders talked, when the USS *Illinois*, a *Virginia*-class nuclear attack submarine, encountered a PLAN South Sea Fleet *Yuan*-class diesel-electric attack submarine off the Riau Archipelago northeast of Singapore. The *Illinois* had picked up the Chinese sub on September 22 and quietly shadowed it for two days before being discovered in turn by its Chinese quarry. Having received information of the submarine attack on the *Liaoning*, the Chinese assumed they were an active target and flooded and opened their torpedo tubes. At that point, the *Illinois* launched a single Mk-48 torpedo that destroyed the Chinese sub. By the time the South Sea Fleet realized their sub was missing on September 29, the inertia of the political agreement between Washington and Beijing was too strong to overcome, and Chinese authorities ordered all forces to adhere to the cease-fire, which had been in effect for four full days.

THE AFTERMATH

The Negotiations and Agreement

Since Congress had not declared war, President Newsom could negotiate and make a settlement directly with Xi Jinping, without having to seek congressional approval. Further, since no territory had been taken by either side, the two leaders agreed to ratify the military status quo at the time of the cease-fire and avoid bringing in diplomats. The commander of US Indo-Pacific Command met the chief of the Joint Staff Department of the PLA's Central Military Commission in Singapore on September 26 and reached an agreement on a permanent cease-fire on September 28.

By the terms of the agreement, each side agreed to inform the other of naval and air activities taking place in the Yellow, East, and South China Seas; the US would notify Beijing of any passage of US naval ships through the South China Sea, while China would undertake to "limit" but not cease its naval activities in the East China Sea to a line extending south from Jeju Island off the southern tip of the Korean Peninsula to approximately 25 degrees north latitude, whence the line would swing southwestward toward Taiwan, bypassing the Senkaku Islands. This would be referred to by both countries as the ECS Median Line.

Further, the US recognized Chinese control over the Spratly and Paracel island chains in the South China Sea, and acknowledged China's "historic interests" in the South China Sea. For its part, the PRC promised never to invade or attack Japan, provided Japan refrained from interfering with peaceful Chinese military activities in the East China Sea. A secret codicil, revealed five years later, contained an American promise to end all military and intelligence aid to Taiwan, effectively killing off the 1979 Taiwan Relations Act.

After the agreement was made public, President Newsom delivered a major address at the Cato Institute think tank in Washington, DC, outlining substantial changes to America's role in the Pacific. He announced a withdrawal of US naval, ground, and air forces from Japan to Guam and Hawaii; the US would leave a token force of one F-16 squadron and two DDGs in Japan but withdraw completely from Okinawa. Enhanced military aid to Japan and full intelligence sharing along the lines of the "Five Eyes" arrangement would be implemented to maintain a strong alliance. In the interests of maintaining peace on the Korean Peninsula, the US Army would maintain a force of 7,000 soldiers—3,500 of them in combat units—down from a prewar total of 28,000, all of them to be located in Busan, on the southern tip of South Korea.

Seeking to reassure America's allies, Newsom reiterated that America's extended deterrence commitments, the so-called nuclear umbrella, would remain in force. He also ordered Defense Secretary Flournoy to submit plans to build up naval and air facilities on Guam and Oahu. Despite public opposition in both locales, land requisition soon expanded the US military's footprint on both islands. In their totality, Newsom's policy shifts caused an uproar among mainstream foreign policy experts, while being applauded on both the progressive left and isolationist right of the political spectrum. The greater geopolitical impact was felt in the emergence of three blocs in the Indo-Pacific.

The Emergence of Three Geopolitical Blocs in East Asia

Within months, or perhaps weeks, after the cease-fire and the announcement of Newsom's new policy, three distinct blocs had begun to form in the region. The first bloc was composed of a rump grouping of US alliances in the region. Japan and Australia remained allied with the United States, though not without significant changes to long-standing security policy. Within six months of Newsom's announcement, Japan had announced the imposition of a national draft for all eighteen- to twenty-five-year-olds for a period of three years; in addition, Tokyo's new National Defense Program Guidelines revealed a $200 billion plan to introduce autonomous systems into all of Japan's combat services, as well as the formation of a cyber warfare command. With only a token US force left in Japan, all US-Japan military exercises were canceled. Press reports by left-wing activist groups suggested that Tokyo had embarked on a secret nuclear weapons program on the northern island of Hokkaido, and that plans were under way to build several nuclear ballistic missile submarines to ensure a survivable counterstrike capability. While left-wing Japanese groups, again supported by Chinese intelligence and United Front operatives, demanded outreach to Beijing, Japan's conservative government reiterated its commitment to the modified alliance with Washington, though public opinion polls indicated that the government might lose its parliamentary majority to the liberal opposition.

Australia announced no change in its posture toward the United States but reiterated calls for full freedom of navigation throughout the Indo-Pacific. Canberra stated that it would be willing to port US Navy ships and expand facilities at the Royal Australian Air Force's Darwin base for the use of US bombers and fighters. Canberra's offer, however, was not immediately acted upon by

Washington, which instead announced that it would host Australian units for joint exercises in Hawaii on a semiannual basis. In mid-October, Newsom and the Philippines president announced that the US alliance with the Philippines would be restricted to political cooperation and economic aid, and that the United States would lose access to any Philippine military bases, effectively ending US security guarantees to Manila and canceling annual defense exercises such as Balikatan.

The second bloc, headed by China, re-created a large portion of the traditional Sinic state system. Taiwan moved first, announcing the week after Newsom's address that it had entered a "new era" in cross-strait relations, whereby Beijing had assured Taipei of a "one country–two systems" arrangement that would preserve Taiwan's autonomous status. China would, however, control the island's foreign policy through a new coordination group, and the two capitals announced in October the formation of an exclusive economic partnership, expanding the 2010 Economic Cooperation Framework Agreement. Taipei agreed to begin downsizing its military into a militia designed to maintain public order, act as a coast guard, and monitor airspace over the island. It further agreed to cease all foreign weapons purchases (thereby making irrelevant the secret US promise to China to stop selling arms to Taiwan).

In what became known as the "St. Valentine's Day Massacre," Seoul announced in mid-February 2026 that it was withdrawing from the US-ROK alliance and was entering into a military "friendship pact" with China, whereby Beijing would undertake to ensure peace and stability on the peninsula. The remaining US troops (seven thousand) would be withdrawn by April Fool's Day 2027, and PLAN vessels would be accorded routine porting privileges at Inchon and Busan. It was unclear whether the Newsom administration was aware of Seoul's plans, despite high-level diplomatic talks that had been ongoing since the September ceasefire. This surprise was followed by the promulgation of a formal alliance between North Korea and China, with DPRK forces joining the PLA in joint naval and air exercises, while Seoul and

Pyongyang agreed to establish joint military liaison offices in each capital under the supervision of PLA officers.

Initially, it appeared as though China was the nearly unambiguous victor in the Littoral War, but it soon became clear that Beijing's new allies were largely unwilling and resentful partners who felt they had no other choice but to throw in their lot with China. Taiwanese grassroots groups regularly protested against the alliance with China, despite a crackdown authorized by a new public safety law. More ominously, politicians from both the Democratic Progressive and Kuomintang political parties in Taiwan increasingly saw that Xi Jinping intended to formally annex the island before his retirement in 2032, and they began to plot ways to frustrate Beijing's designs.

Even more resistant were the Koreas, which before long began to discuss the formation of a peninsular unity movement that would allow for a united front to deal with China. Anti-Chinese demonstrations regularly took place in major cities throughout the peninsula, and the two Korean capitals soon learned that they could beg out of joint military exercises with the Chinese by claiming lack of funds, unstable public opinion, or (in the South) looming elections.

The third bloc to emerge out of the Littoral War revived the Cold War–era Nonaligned Movement, declaring a comprehensive neutrality between the US and Chinese blocs, opening itself to trade with both, and—depending on the country—allowing mutual military access to both great powers, though in practice this meant far more access for the PLA than for the US military. The nonaligned bloc was centered on the ten members of the Association of Southeast Asian Nations (ASEAN), headquartered in Jakarta, Indonesia. Some members of ASEAN traditionally had extensive ties with the United States, whether as ally or partner.

While not a formal ally, Singapore nonetheless had had the closest relations with Washington of all Southeast Asian nations prior to the war. In the aftermath, however, Singapore joined its ASEAN partners and moved to distance itself from the United States, announcing that henceforth only noncombat US naval vessels would be allowed porting privileges, while US combat aircraft could no longer land at Changi Air Base. Similarly, the US ally Thailand also chose its ASEAN neighbors. The military-backed junta that had ruled Thailand since its overthrow of yet another popularly elected government in 2022 announced it was suspending cooperation with the US military, while urging both Washington and Moscow to provide further development assistance to help "stabilize" the domestic economy so that parliamentary elections could be scheduled at the "earliest possible date." The Philippines, for its part, welcomed the economic and political aid provided by the revised alliance agreed to with Newsom, but Manila openly sided with ASEAN in proclaiming itself a neutral, having already lost the remainder of its Spratly Islands claims in the weeks after the war, when PLA units took over all contested territory in the chain.

The nonaligned bloc found two champions in India and Russia. Both New Delhi and Moscow took advantage of the trifurcation of East Asia to advance their interests. India became the diplomatic and economic champion of the nonaligned nations, enhancing ties and even proposing maritime partnerships that would see Indian naval vessels escort the merchant ships of Southeast Asian nations. For its part, Russia offered deep discounts on military hardware to all nations pledging to maintain a nonaligned status. Moscow quickly became the major arms dealer in the region and offered Russian armed forces personnel to train nations in their new purchases.

Other global powers, primarily the Europeans, quickly lost the appetite to play any significant role in the Indo-Pacific. Once Beijing announced on October 1 that it would ensure freedom of navigation for all merchant vessels through its "zone of control" in the South China Sea, the European Commission stated that it recognized China's control over the body of water, and would work with the PLAN to file shipping manifests and routes of transit. The British government, which had begun plans to build a new base in Singapore, following on then defense secretary Gavin Williamson's December 2018 announcement, canceled the project and announced that all future planned transits of the HMS *Queen Elizabeth* (R08) aircraft carrier through the South and East China Seas would be postponed.

THE LESSONS

Almost immediately after the announcement of the permanent cease-fire, analysts in the United States began debating the lessons of the war. While few interpretations were universally accepted, several key insights were generally seen as correct.

First, the origins of the war were years in the making. While historians cautioned against assuming that war was inevitable, or that the United States and China were fated to fight, observers agreed that years of deteriorating relations were a precondition to war. As suspicion grew in each country about the other, as working relations became more strained and formal, as the two eyed each other as the major threat each faced, both Washington and Beijing gave up on attempting to establish mechanisms to resolve the growing differences between them. Instead, each increasingly sought to justify actions that increased tensions and suspicion.

American analysts, however, were largely united in seeing China as the aggressor in the years leading up to the war. While the goal of US policy toward China since the 1970s had been to integrate it into the global economic and political system, Beijing increasingly chafed at what it considered to be restrictions on its freedom of action outside its borders. Instead of gaining confidence in dealing with the world, Chinese leaders, and especially Xi Jinping, saw enemies all around China; indeed, as US observers pointed out, in the years before the war, China had disputes with almost all of its neighbors, particularly maritime ones in the East and South China Seas. It was China, moreover, that built up a military designed to target US strengths in the region, precisely at the time when Washington was eager to make China the de facto number two in the global hierarchy. Finally, it was Beijing that intimidated and harassed its neighbors, threatened Taiwan, took maritime territory when possible, and built and militarized island bases in the South China Sea during the 2010s. Ultimately, it was aggressive Chinese actions on September 8–9, 2025, that led to the accidents which precipitated conflict.

Second, all analysts and historians recognized the crucial role of contingency in the outbreak of hostilities. Because US and Chinese ships and planes were increasingly in proximity to each other, accidents were more likely to happen, especially given the aggressive nature of Chinese ship drivers and pilots. The 2001 EP-3E incident was a harbinger of the kind of accident that could throw relations into a tailspin. As it turned out, the two unconnected incidents on September 8 were enough to tip the balance toward conflict, given high tensions and the lack of deconfliction between US and PLA forces in the skies and on the sea. In short, the two nations stumbled into a war neither wanted.

In addition, later on in the conflict, the disabling of the *Liaoning* by a JMSDF attack submarine on September 22 introduced a wild card into combat operations. The Chinese retaliatory attack on the USS *Gerald Ford* had the potential to cause the war to spiral out of control, leading to US attacks on mainland missile launch sites, communications nodes, ports, airfields, and the like. These, in turn, would almost certainly have resulted in Chinese counterattacks on US territory, including Guam and Hawaii, and possibly San Diego. The next step might well have been limited nuclear exchanges (this will be discussed further in the fifth point, below).

Third, probably because the two came into armed conflict accidentally, rather than through intent on either side, neither was sure just how far hostilities would develop, nor how far they themselves wanted to go. Rather than activating full war plans, each side initially concentrated on the narrow site of the accidents, combining rescue operations with attempts to clear the other country's forces from the vicinity. Washington hoped that minimum deterrence would initially suffice to send signals to Beijing that US forces would not surrender its position in eastern Asian waters without a fight. For its part, Beijing, though committed to achieving domination in Asia's seas, hesitated to commit to a horizontal escalation of hostilities to land-based targets, fearing the impact of retaliatory responses on Chinese soil. Severe criticism of Xi Jinping's decision not to launch ballistic missile attacks against US air bases in Japan discounted his focus on achieving victory solely on the immediate battlefield, as opposed to risking a larger US retaliation for bombing targets in an allied country. This initial hesitancy on both sides led to a gradual widening of conflict, but each escalation was linked directly to the specific action that preceded it. This kept the scale of the conflict limited in its early days, which in turn shaped the operational response (see a fuller discussion of limited war aims in the fifth point, below).

Fourth, the actual course of combat operations largely followed the insights of geopolitical analysts Halford Mackinder and Nicholas John Spykman.[42] Both Mackinder and Spykman stressed the crucial importance of the "rimlands": the littoral and adjacent maritime space, which Spykman called the "marginal seas." The rimlands are the vital areas that must be controlled, given their importance in populations, industrial production, and access to the continental interior and its resources. However, to control the rimlands, the inner seas must be dominated by one power. In other words, it is in the marginal or inner seas that the struggle for mastery takes place, between what Mackinder called the "inner crescent" of the littoral mainland and the "outer crescent" of the peninsular littoral (in this case, formed by Japan, Taiwan, the Philippines, and other nations of Southeast Asia).

US and Chinese combat operations focused on winning the war in the marginal seas, along the littorals, and not on expanding combat either to the continent (in the case of the United States) or to third countries like Japan (in the case of China). Naval forces were concentrated at key choke points or along vital sea lines of communication, such as the Miyako and Jeju Straits, which formed the hinges between the East and South China Seas. Taiwan also played a central geopolitical role here, and its declaration of neutrality was a major strategic gain for China. Similarly, the Battles of the Batanes, Ryukyus, and Santiago Island all underscored the importance of the littorals and strategic transit points.

Both US and Chinese forces faced constraints due to distance in the theater of operations. US naval forces in the region were inadequate to prosecute combat operations without help, but the amount of steaming time from (a) Japan to the Spratlys, (b) Hawaii to Japan, and (c) San Diego to Japan meant that US forces were stretched too thin to fight effectively in the South China Sea. Moreover, US land-based and naval air forces could not operate at enough range to maintain persistent presence over the battle sites in the South China Sea. They were dominant in all air-to-air encounters when they were located within stand-off missile range, such as at the Battle of the Batanes and Santiago Island, but were vulnerable to SAMs fired from PLAN destroyers. The subsequent disabling of the *Gerald Ford* and the threat to aerial tankers, however, forced US forces to limit air cover after the initial days of battle.

On the other hand, the Chinese naval forces benefited from proximity to bases on the mainland and Hainan, as well as in the Paracel and Spratly Islands. Yet Chinese air forces were bested by their US opponents, and China also lost effective air cover after the early days of the war. Chinese military officials did not hesitate to use land-based missiles, especially DF-21D ASBMs against large US targets, and effectively used swarm missile attacks from smaller Type 22 missile patrol boats both in the Taiwan Strait and off Santiago Island.

Given the relatively brief duration of the war and its limitation to force-on-force battles in the littorals, neither side faced severe logistical constraints, such as lack of ordnance or fuel. American land-based and naval air forces did face a drawdown of ordnance, due to the relatively limited carrying capacity of F-35s in stealth mode. Along with routine mechanical problems, this would have wound up further limiting the effectiveness of US air operations had the conflict continued for several more weeks.

Fifth, crucially, neither Washington nor Beijing was willing to risk or felt prepared for a full war. Rather, even after the loss of their aircraft carriers, both sides showed restraint during combat operations, as noted in the third point, above. The key moment

of restraint for the US was to avoid attacks on the Chinese mainland, especially missile sites, after the launching of DF-21Ds on
two occasions against the *Gerald Ford*. Similarly, the Chinese did
not target US air and naval bases on Okinawa, Guam, Hawaii,
or the Japanese main island of Honshu, even when the US Indo-
Pacific Command began moving assets from those bases to the
area of the campaign. Most surprisingly to US war planners, the
PLA conducted relatively limited electronic warfare operations,
perhaps out of fear that expansion of electronic warfare to the US
mainland would result in similar attacks and significant disruption at home; moreover, US workarounds, primarily the ship-
launched balloon communications network, partially blunted the
effectiveness of China's initial electronic warfare salvoes. No sat-
isfactory explanation was ever offered for the Chinese restraint,
but suspicions remained rife that Xi Jinping was not willing to
risk any domestic disruption that could mutate into anti-CCP
movements, especially if the Americans could be checkmated
early in the conflict.

Instead, each side limited itself to force-on-force encounters in
the littoral seas and skies, confident of its ability to cripple the forward forces of the other and thereby impose an unacceptable cost
in making the other commit further military assets. The United
States did surge forces from Japan, Hawaii, and San Diego, but the
Japan-based forces were checked at sea, while the Chinese decided
to propose a cease-fire before US naval forces surged from Hawaii
and San Diego could reach the combat zones. From a political perspective, Beijing was willing to cease combat operations to consolidate its significant gains, while the United States accepted its
strategic losses and did not want to widen the war, which could
have resulted in further defeats, especially once the effectiveness
of the Chinese DF-21D and swarm missile attacks was proven.
Instead, Washington decided that a reduced military presence in
the region, centered on its alliances with Japan and Australia, was
a better outcome than betting on the fortunes of war.

With each combatant willing, therefore, to limit future operations to preserve gains or prevent further loss, the political

conditions were created for a geopolitical settlement that resulted in the emergence of the three blocs discussed in the previous section. Beijing concluded that its victory provided momentum whereby it could continue to squeeze the rump American alliance network and steadily put pressure on the nonaligned bloc. Publicly, Chinese officials repeatedly maintained that Beijing considered the diplomatic solution as merely "temporary," and that China would not rule out further action to follow up on its gains, but it failed to put into motion any plans to take advantage of its success. Moreover, as discussed, Beijing soon discovered that its unwilling allies required the investment of Chinese political, economic, and military capital, which restricted Beijing's freedom of action postbellum.

The United States limited its strategic goals to protecting Japan and ensuring that it could operate in part of East Asia's marginal seas (namely, the eastern portion of the East China Sea) as well as beyond the outer crescent of Japan. This allowed for the possibility of power projection into the inner seas and littorals in a future crisis, but turned the US largely into an offshore balancer, with its forces concentrated in Hawaii and on Guam. That made its remaining alliances, with Japan and Australia, inherently weaker than before the war.

The end result was a trifurcation of the Indo-Pacific into three geopolitical blocs, two of which—the Chinese and American—were mutually antagonistic, while the third, nonaligned block maneuvered for advantage between the other two. A cold peace settled on East Asia, reducing, though not eliminating, intraregional trade, while multilateral diplomatic mechanisms such as those sponsored by ASEAN became arenas for rhetorical combat between the blocs. A sharp drop in Sino-US trade rocked both countries, with the United States entering a recession that lasted three years, while reports of widespread demonstrations in China hinted at pervasive domestic unrest. Trade slowly stabilized between the two, but some of the nonaligned countries, particularly India, Vietnam, and Malaysia, retooled their economies to supplant China in the global supply chain, leading to a boost in their exports to America and Europe.

As the cold peace settled on the region, the Chinese and American blocs settled down into a prolonged contest for influence in Asia. Beijing continued its military buildup, though at a slower pace than during the 2000s and 2010s, given its economic slowdown. American defense planners increased their reliance on unmanned systems, hypersonics, underwater systems, and cyberwar capabilities. Both increased their espionage activities and conducted a regular military cat-and-mouse game in the skies and on the waters of the region. As of this writing, the two antagonists have so far avoided outright conflict and a repeat of the Littoral War, perhaps as much through luck as through a wariness on both sides to stumble once again into armed conflict.

RECOMMENDATIONS FOR FURTHER READING

To understand the broader geopolitical context in which a Sino-American clash might evolve, particularly in light of the economic, political, demographic, and security problems in Asia, see Michael R. Auslin, *The End of the Asian Century: War, Stagnation, and the Risks to the World's Most Dynamic Region* (New Haven: Yale University Press, 2017). Though largely out of fashion these days, the study of geopolitics is crucial for considering the national interests of both the United States and China; a classic text is Nicholas Spykman's *America's Strategy in World Politics: The United States and the Balance of Power* (New York: Harcourt, Brace and Company, 1942). To imagine how an actual littoral war would play out, the basics of naval warfare, along with a useful future combat scenario, the standard text is Wayne P. Hughes Jr. and Robert P. Girrier, *Fleet Tactics and Naval Operations*, third edition (Annapolis, MD: Naval Institute Press, 2018).

Creating a future scenario also depends on understanding the past. Two books on the Pacific War between Japan and America are useful: Gordon W. Prange's *Miracle at Midway* (New York: McGraw-Hill, 1982) looks at the confluence of strategy and contingency in military operations, while Dan van der Vat's *The Pacific Campaign: The US-Japanese Naval War 1941–1945* (New York: Simon & Schuster, 1991) gives a broad overview of politics, strategy, and tactics. Finally, assumptions about the possibility of conflict between China and America in the Pacific rest in part on knowing how the Chinese military and especially navy are evolving. Some well-regarded books to start with are Bernard D. Cole, *The Great Wall at Sea: China's Navy in the Twenty-First Century*, second edition (Annapolis, MD: Naval Institute Press, 2012); Toshi Yoshihara and James R. Holmes, *Red Star over the Pacific: China's Rise and the Challenge to U.S. Maritime Strategy*, revised edition (Annapolis, MD: Naval Institute Press, 2018); and Andrew S. Erickson and Ryan D. Martinson, eds., *China's Maritime Gray Zone Operations*, Studies in Chinese Maritime Development (Annapolis, MD: Naval Institute Press, 2019).

NOTES

1. Robert Ross, "The 1995–96 Taiwan Strait Confrontation: Coercion, Credibility, and the Use of Force," *International Security* 24, no. 2 (Fall 2000): 87.
2. "Cox Report, 1999," USC US-China Institute, https://china.usc.edu/cox-report-1999; "APT1: Exposing One of China's Cyber Espionage Units," Mandiant, https://www.fireeye.com/content/dam/fireeye-www/services/pdfs/mandiant-apt1-report.pdf.
3. "Remarks by President Obama and President Xi Jinping of the People's Republic of China after Bilateral Meeting," White House Office of the Press Secretary, June 8, 2013, https://obamawhitehouse.archives.gov/the-press-office/2013/06/08/remarks-president-obama-and-president-xi-jinping-peoples-republic-china-.
4. Tom Phillips, "Barack Obama 'Deliberately Snubbed' by Chinese in Chaotic Arrival at G20," *The Guardian*, September 4, 2016.
5. Hillary Rodham Clinton, "Remarks at Press Availability," July 23, 2010, US Department of State, https://2009-2017.state.gov/secretary/20092013clinton/rm/2010/07/145095.htm.
6. "Pivot to the Pacific? The Obama Administration's 'Rebalancing' toward Asia," Congressional Research Service, March 28, 2012,

https://fas.org/sgp/crs/natsec/R42448.pdf; Johnathan Marcus, "Leon Panetta: US to Deploy 60% of Navy Fleet to Pacific," *BBC News*, June 2, 2012.

7. Edward Wong, "Chinese Military Seeks to Extend Its Naval Power," *New York Times*, April 23, 2010.

8. Jane Perlez, "American and Chinese Navy Ships Nearly Collided in South China Sea," *New York Times*, December 14, 2013; Elisabeth Rosenthal and David Sanger, "US Plane in China after It Collides with Chinese Jet," *New York Times*, April 2, 2001.

9. Lolita Baldor, "Report: China Has Reclaimed 3,200 Acres in South China Sea," *Associated Press*, May 13, 2016.

10. Jane Perlez, "Tribunal Rejects Beijing's Claims in South China Sea," *New York Times*, July 12, 2016.

11. Sam LaGrone, "China Upset over 'Unprofessional' U.S. South China Sea Freedom of Navigation Operation," *USNI News*, January 31, 2016.

12. The National Security Strategy can be found at https://www.white house.gov/wp-content/uploads/2017/12/NSS-Final-12-18-2017-0905-2.pdf.

13. "'Prepare for War': China's President Xi Jinping Tells Advisers of South China Sea," *New Zealand Herald*, October 28, 2018.

14. This section owes much to Bernard D. Cole, "The People's Liberation Army in 2020–30: Focused on Regional Issues," in *The Chinese People's Liberation Army in 2025*, ed. Roy Kamphausen and David Lai (Carlisle, PA: US Army War College Press, 2015), 165–206. See also Rick Joe, "Predicting the Chinese Navy of 2030," *The Diplomat*, February 15, 2019.

15. Cole, "The People's Liberation Army," 183–86.

16. Extrapolated from projected figures. See Department of Defense, "Annual Report to Congress: Military and Security Developments Involving the People's Republic of China 2018," May 16, 2018, 33, https://media .defense.gov/2018/Aug/16/2001955282/-1/-1/1/2018-CHINA-MILITARY -POWER-REPORT.PDF.

17. Department of Defense, "Annual Report to Congress," 70.

18. Based on current US Navy force levels. See "The United States Seventh Fleet," Commander, US 7th Fleet website, https://www.c7f.navy.mil/ About-Us/Facts-Sheet.

19. "About the United States Third Fleet," Commander, US 3rd Fleet website, https://www.c3f.navy.mil/About-Us/Fact-Sheets/Article/ 638101/about-us.

20. Extrapolated from current US Air Force deployment figures. See "Pacific Air Forces," October 9, 2015, US Air Force website, https://www .af.mil/About-Us/Fact-Sheets/Display/Article/104483/pacific-air-forces.

21. See Kerry K. Gershaneck and James E. Fanell, "How China Began World War III in the South China Sea," *National Interest*, March 26, 2019.

22. Martin Petty, "Exclusive: At Strategic Shoal, China Asserts Power through Control, and Concessions," *Reuters*, April 9, 2017, https://www.reuters.com/article/us-southchinasea-china-philippines-exclu/exclusive-at-strategic-shoal-china-asserts-power-through-control-and-concessions-idUSKBN17B124.

23. "Mutual Defense Treaty between the United States and the Republic of the Philippines; August 30, 1951," available at the Yale Law School Lillian Goldman Law Library website, http://avalon.law.yale.edu/20th_century/philo01.asp.

24. Barbara Starr, Ryan Browne, and Brad Lendon, "Chinese Warship in 'Unsafe' Encounter with US Destroyer, amid Rising US-China Tensions," *CNN Politics*, October 1, 2018.

25. Willy Lo-Lap Lam, "Xi Jinping Warns against the 'Black Swans' and 'Gray Rhinos' of a Possible Color Revolution," *China Brief*, February 20, 2019, https://jamestown.org/program/china-brief-early-warning-xi-jinping-warns-against-the-black-swans-and-gray-rhinos-of-a-possible-color-revolution.

26. Barbara Demick, "In a Disputed Reef, Philippines Sees Face of Chinese Domination," *Los Angeles Times*, May 14, 2013.

27. Khan Vu, "Vietnam Protests to China over South China Sea Boat Sinking," *Reuters*, March 21, 2019, https://www.reuters.com/article/us-vietnam-southchinasea/vietnam-protests-to-china-over-south-china-sea-boat-sinking-idUSKCN1R307O.

28. Gordon Lubold and Jeremy Page, "U.S. Ship Sails near Disputed South China Sea Islands in Challenge to Beijing," *Wall Street Journal*, January 7, 2019.

29. Bart Elias and Ian Rinehart, "China's Air Defense Identification Zone (ADIZ)," Congressional Research Service, January 30, 2015, https://fas.org/sgp/crs/row/R43894.pdf.

30. Rosenthal and Sanger, "US Plane in China after It Collides with Chinese Jet."

31. Michael Fabey, "U.S. Navy's EP-3 Replacement Plan Still Raises Concerns," *Aerospace Daily and Defense Report*, May 12, 2016.

32. Starr, Browne, and Lendon, "Chinese Warship in 'Unsafe' Encounter."

33. Mari Yamaguchi, "Japan Shows Video of Alleged Radar Lock-On by SKorea Warship," *ABC News*, December 28, 2018.

34. "Littoral Combat Ship (LCS)," Department of Defense's Director, Operational Test and Evaluation, https://www.dote.osd.mil/pub/reports/FY2017/pdf/navy/2017lcs.pdf.

35. "An Accounting of China's Deployments to the Spratly Islands," Asia Maritime Transparency Initiative, May 9, 2018, https://amti.csis.org/accounting-chinas-deployments-spratly-islands.

36. On US base vulnerability, see Tanner Greer, "US Bases in Japan Are Sitting Ducks," *Foreign Policy*, September 4, 2019, https://foreignpolicy.com/2019/09/04/american-bases-in-japan-are-sitting-ducks; see also Oriana Skylar Mastro and Ian Easton, "Risk and Resiliency: China's Emerging Air Base Strike Threat," Project 2049 Institute, November 8, 2017, https://project2049.net/2017/11/08/risk-and-resiliency-chinas-emerging-air-base-strike-threat; Thomas Shugart and Javier Gonzalez, "First Strike: China's Missile Threat to US Bases in Asia, Center for a New American Security," June 2017, https://s3.amazonaws.com/files.cnas.org/documents/CNASReport-FirstStrike-Final.pdf?mtime=20170626140814.

37. Elizabeth McLaughlin and Luis Martinez, "US B-52 Flies over Disputed Islands in the South China Sea," *ABC News*, March 5, 2019.

38. I would like to thank Toshi Yoshihara for highlighting this point to me and introducing the concept of "minimum deterrence" from Donald Kagan.

39. "Anti-Japan Protests across China over Islands Dispute," *BBC News*, August 19, 2012.

40. See Gerry Shih and Emily Rauhala, "Angry over Campus Speech by Uighur Activist, Chinese Students in Canada Contact Their Consulate, Film Presentation," *Washington Post*, February 2, 2019. On the United Front Work Department, see "China's Overseas United Front Work," US-China Economic and Security Review Commission, August 24, 2018, https://www.uscc.gov/sites/default/files/Research/China%27s%20Overseas%20United%20Front%20Work%20-%20Background%20and%20Implications%20for%20US_final_0.pdf.

41. Chris Buckley and Chris Horton, "Xi Jinping Warns Taiwan That Unification Is the Goal and Force Is an Option," *New York Times*, January 1, 2019.

42. Halford Mackinder, "The Geographical Pivot of History," in *Geographical Journal* 23, no. 4 (April 1904): 421–37; Nicholas John Spykman, *The Geography of the Peace* (New York: Harcourt, Brace, 1944).

ABOUT THE AUTHORS

David L. Berkey, a research fellow at the Hoover Institution and member of the executive board of the Working Group on the Role of Military History in Contemporary Conflict, works with Victor Davis Hanson in the fields of classics and military history. Before coming to Hoover, Berkey was a professor in the Department of History at California State University, Fresno. He holds a BA in international studies from Johns Hopkins University and a PhD in classics and ancient history from Yale University. Berkey has studied at both the American Academy in Rome and the American School of Classical Studies at Athens.

Victor Davis Hanson is the Martin and Illie Anderson Senior Fellow at the Hoover Institution and chairs the Military History Working Group. He is an American scholar of ancient and modern warfare and has been a commentator on contemporary politics for various media outlets. He is a professor emeritus of classics at California State University, Fresno, and the annual Wayne and Marcia Buske Distinguished Visiting Fellow in History at Hillsdale College since 2004. Hanson was awarded the National Humanities Medal in 2007 by President George W. Bush and was a recipient of the Bradley Prize in 2008. Hanson is also a farmer and a critic of social trends related to farming and agrarianism. The author of numerous books, his most recent are *The Second World Wars. How the First Global Conflict Was Fought and Won* and *The Case for Trump*.

Michael R. Auslin is the inaugural Payson J. Treat Distinguished Research Fellow in Contemporary Asia at the Hoover Institution.

A historian by training, he specializes in current and historical US policy in Asia and political and security issues in the Indo-Pacific region. He is the author of *Asia's New Geopolitics: Essays on Reshaping the Indo-Pacific* and the best-selling *The End of the Asian Century: War, Stagnation, and the Risks to the World's Most Dynamic Region*, among other books. He is a longtime contributor to the *Wall Street Journal* and *National Review*, and his writings appear in other leading publications, including *The Atlantic*, *Foreign Affairs*, *Foreign Policy*, and *Politico*. Previously, he was an associate professor of history at Yale University, a resident scholar at the American Enterprise Institute, and a visiting professor at the University of Tokyo.

Edward N. Luttwak works as a contractor for the US Department of Defense and for some treaty allies, and has served as consultant to the White House chief of staff, the US Department of State, and the US Army, Air Force, and Navy. Luttwak also cofounded and heads a conservation cattle ranch in the Amazon. His books, including *The Rise of China vs. The Logic of Strategy*, *The Grand Strategy of the Byzantine Empire*, *The Grand Strategy of the Roman Empire*, and *Strategy: The Logic of War and Peace* have been published in multiple English-language editions and also in twenty-three other languages, including Arabic, Chinese, Japanese, Hebrew, Korean, and Russian. He has also published other books in Italian and in Japanese, and has a number of honorary as well as academic degrees.

Peter R. Mansoor, colonel, US Army (retired), is the General Raymond E. Mason Jr. Chair of Military History at Ohio State University. A 1982 distinguished graduate of the United States Military Academy at West Point, he earned his doctorate from Ohio State. He assumed his current position after a twenty-six-year career in the US Army that included two combat tours, the first as a brigade commander in Baghdad and his final duty as executive officer to General David Petraeus, commander of Multi-National Force–Iraq. His latest works are *Surge: My Journey with General David Petraeus and the Remaking of the Iraq War* (2013), a history of the surge in Iraq in 2007–8; and *Grand*

Strategy and Military Alliances (2016) and *The Culture of Military Organizations* (2019), both coedited with Williamson Murray.

Paul A. Rahe holds the Charles O. Lee and Louise K. Lee Chair in the Western Heritage at Hillsdale College, where he is a professor of history. He is the author of *Republics Ancient and Modern: Classical Republicanism and the American Revolution; Against Throne and Altar: Machiavelli and Political Theory under the English Republic; Montesquieu and the Logic of Liberty: War, Religion, Commerce, Climate, Terrain, Technology; Uneasiness of Mind, the Spirit of Political Vigilance and the Foundations of the Modern Republic; Soft Despotism, Democracy's Drift: Montesquieu, Rousseau, Tocqueville, and the Modern Prospect; The Spartan Regime: Its Character, Origins, and Grand Strategy;* and *The Grand Strategy of Classical Sparta: The Persian Challenge. Sparta's First Attic War: The Grand Strategy of Classical Sparta, 478–446 BC* was awarded the 2019 Strategic Forecasting Prize for the Best Book in Geopolitical Analysis. His latest book—*Sparta's Second Attic War: The Grand Strategy of Classical Sparta, 446–418 BC*—will be published in August 2020. Professor Rahe writes on contemporary politics and culture for the website Ricochet.

Andrew Roberts studied modern history at Caius College, Cambridge, from which he received a PhD. He has written *Salisbury: Victorian Titan* (which won the Wolfson Prize), *Masters and Commanders* (International Churchill Society Book Award), *The Storm of War: A New History of the Second World War* (British Army Military Book of the Year Award), *Napoleon the Great* (Grand Prix of the Fondation Napoléon and the Los Angeles Times Biography Prize), *Churchill: Walking with Destiny* (Council on Foreign Relations Arthur Ross Prize), and *Leadership in War: Essential Lessons from Those Who Made History.* He is the Roger and Martha Mertz Visiting Research Fellow at the Hoover Institution at Stanford University, the Lehrman Institute Distinguished Lecturer at the New-York Historical Society, a visiting professor at the Department of War Studies at King's College London, and a fellow of the Royal Society of Literature and the Royal Historical Society. He lives in London.

Barry Strauss, Bryce and Edith M. Bowmar Professor in Humanistic Studies, Cornell University, is a military historian with a focus on ancient Greece and Rome. His books have been translated into fifteen languages. His latest book, *Ten Caesars: Roman Emperors from Augustus to Constantine*, has been hailed as a "superb summation of four centuries of Roman history, a masterpiece of compression" (*Wall Street Journal*). His *Battle of Salamis: The Naval Encounter That Saved Greece—and Western Civilization* was named one of the best books of 2004 by the *Washington Post*. His *Masters of Command: Alexander, Hannibal, Caesar and the Genius of Leadership* was named one of the best books of 2012 by Bloomberg. In 2019–20 he was distinguished visiting professor at the Naval Postgraduate School and a visiting fellow at the Hoover Institution. In recognition of his scholarship, he was named an Honorary Citizen of Salamis, Greece.

WORKING GROUP ON THE ROLE OF MILITARY HISTORY
IN CONTEMPORARY CONFLICT

The Working Group on the Role of Military History in Contemporary Conflict examines how knowledge of past military operations can influence contemporary public-policy decisions concerning current conflicts.

As the very name of the Hoover Institution attests, military history lies at the very core of our dedication to the study of "War, Revolution, and Peace." Indeed, the precise mission statement of the Hoover Institution includes the following promise: "The overall mission of this Institution is, from its records, to recall the voice of experience against the making of war, and by the study of these records and their publication, to recall man's endeavors to make and preserve peace, and to sustain for America the safeguards of the American way of life." From its origins as a library and archive, the Hoover Institution has evolved into one of the foremost research centers in the world for policy formation and pragmatic analysis. It is with this tradition in mind that the Working Group on the Role of Military History in Contemporary Conflict has set its agenda—reaffirming the Hoover Institution's dedication to historical research in light of contemporary challenges, and in particular, reinvigorating the national study of military history as an asset to foster and enhance our national security. By bringing together a diverse group of distinguished military historians, security analysts, and military veterans and practitioners, the working group seeks to examine the conflicts of the past as critical lessons for the present.

The careful study of military history offers a way of analyzing modern war and peace that is often underappreciated in this age of technological determinism. Yet the result leads to a more in-depth and dispassionate understanding of contemporary wars, one that explains how particular military successes and failures of the past can be often germane, sometimes misunderstood, or occasionally irrelevant in the context of the present.

The working group is chaired by Victor Davis Hanson with counsel from Bruce S. Thornton and David L. Berkey, along with collaboration from the group's distinguished scholars, military historians, analysts, journalists, and military officers.

INDEX

Index

195